THE STINGER

D. E. Ritterbusch

ECLECTIC BLUE PUBLISHING
805 MAULDIN ROAD
STE 2007
GREENVILLE SC 29607

2022

ECLECTIC BLUE PUBLISHING
805 MAULDIN ROAD
STE 2007
GREENVILLE SC 29607

EclecticBluePublishing@gmail.com
423-202-0937

Cover art by Richard James Olsen
Wall LXXVII (77) state2, oil, 37x 47 in, 1992-2005
richard.j.olsen@att.net

By D. E. RITTERBUSCH

Lessons Learned: Poetry of the Vietnam War and its Aftermath

Far From the Temple of Heaven

Tipping Point

ACKNOWLEDGMENTS

Grateful acknowledgment is made to the following publications in which these poems originally appeared and to the editors who subsequently reprinted these poems in their journals or anthologies:

AETHLON: THE JOURNAL OF SPORT LITERATURE: 44; *She Throws Like a Girl; Playing Center in My Forties; Vacations in Northern Wisconsin, 1940's; Ice Bowl; Old Guys Playing Hoops; Water Wolf; Running at Midnight; Running with a Coyote; Sixth Grade Buckets; The Stinger; Lure; The Lake; The Hard Slow Dance of the Pugilist; Popping Up to Second; The Bigger They Are; Aluminum; What Nobody Learns; A Theology of Circumnavigation*

BASEBALLBARD.COM: *Auker's Lament; Poetry and Sports*

CALAPOOYA COLLAGE: *Aluminum II*

DEADLY WRITER'S PATROL: *Boundary Waters*

ELEVEN WISCONSIN POETS: *In Northern Ontario; Canoe Trip; 44*

ELIXIR: *God Works in Mysterious Ways*

ELYSIAN FIELDS QUARTERLY: THE BASEBALL REVIEW: *from The Adcock Poems: Fred Haney Mismanages History*

FAR FROM THE TEMPLE OF HEAVEN: *Canoeing Quetico, 20 Years After; Sledding with Kerry; She Throws Like a Girl; Vacations in Northern Wisconsin, 1940's; World Series, 1968, Southeast Asia; Foxhead 400; Winter Nudes; The Quarry; Indian Summer Grasshoppers*

FOLIATE OAK LITERARY MAGAZINE: *Fitness*

FREE VERSE: *Old Guys Playing Hoops; Aubade; Winter Nudes*

KENNESAW REVIEW: *The Lake*

LAKE SUPERIOR STATE UNIVERSITY LITERARY REVIEW: *Canoeing Quetico, Twenty Years After; Trophies*

LESSONS LEARNED: *Boundary Waters; Canoe Trip*

LINE DRIVES: 100 CONTEMPORARY BASEBALL POEMS: *World Series, 1968, Southeast Asia*

MADISON CAPITOL NEWS: *The Stinger*

MUSELETTER: *She Throws Like a Girl; Aluminum II*

POETRY: *First Glove*

SOUTH BOSTON LITERARY GAZETTE: *Ice Bowl; The Bigger They Are; Auker's Lament*

VIETNAM WAR GENERATION JOURNAL: *The Outfield Coming Home; Behind the Plate; Playing Baseball in the Army: Company Picnic, 1967; World Series, 1968, Southeast Asia; Something Like a War*

VOICES IN WARTIME: *(Frontline) World Series, 1968, Southeast Asia; The Air Force Plays Baseball Near the South China Sea*

WAR, LITERATURE & THE ARTS: *Something Like a War; Behind the Plate; Playing Baseball in the Army: Company Picnic, 1967; Icebowl; World Series, 1968, Southeast Asia; The Air Force Plays Baseball Near the South China Sea*

WINNING WRITERS: *Mother Teresa Plays Tennis*

WISCONSIN ACADEMY REVIEW: *The Stinger, reprinted in the Waukesha Freeman; The Quarry*

WISCONSIN ACADEMY OF SCIENCES, ARTS AND LETTERS: *First Glove; Lure; Water Wolf*
WISCONSIN FELLOWSHIP OF POETS: *Sledding with Kerry; Garage Day; Indian Summer Grasshoppers*

WISCONSIN POETRY: *44*

WISCONSIN REVIEW: *A Find in the Woods*

WISCONSIN POETRY ONLINE: http://www.wisc.edu/wisacad: *First Glove*

www.midnightangel1308.com: *Behind the Plate; Something Like a War*

http://www.wastelandpoets.com: *First Glove*

www.usafa.af.mil: *Playing Baseball in the Army: Company Picnic, 1967; Something Like a War; World Series, 1968, Southeast Asia*

POETRY AND SPORTS

At a card show in Illinois
the greatest hitters of all time:
McGuire, Griffey, Bonds
and other stars who will sign autographs
for a small fee—everything authenticated,
everything licensed and guaranteed—
like the Sammy Sosa bobble head
doll you get for free
when you purchase your ticket to the show.
This is the principle difference between
poets and sports stars—there is no
T.S. Eliot bobble head doll, no Ezra Pound,
no W.S. Merwin nodding their literary
heads on display, enhancing your décor.
And *Who is this?* your guests would say,
looking at Wallace Stevens bobbling on the mantle.
But I go anyway, despite the prejudice,
and on my way home after the show,
my wallet empty, charge cards maxed,
signed photos and baseballs in the trunk,
I sing *I don't care if it rains or freezes*
long's I got my plastic
Sammy Sosa bobble head doll
sitting on the dashboard of my car.
A memento of the good life,
with poetry or without.

ETERNAL DELIGHT:
A MEDITATION ON SPORTS AND POETRY

Poetry is a strange animal, ancient in its bestiary and mythical in its hold on the human psyche. So, of course, inevitably, it is fraught with prejudices, bias endemic to our nature, hence the request to write a short forward to this collection by persons anticipating the usual objections and renunciations of such a collection as this one concerned as it is with the physical nature of our being. In effect, a defense of poetry, particularly poetry that employs sport as subtext. Our intellectual pursuits are separate from our physical engagements with the world, and in the realm of academia relegated to a loftier position, but yet, in our academic labors, may we not ask if there is not more to this existence than a life of the mind? Perhaps, perhaps not, but such is a false dichotomy, and besides there are so many other objections.

Once, many decades ago in a classroom far, far away, I told my students that we would shortly begin a block of instruction on war poetry. "War poetry," a young woman exhorted, "How can you possibly have poetry about war?" Well, you can, and my experiences as a young Army officer during the primary years of the Vietnam War gave rise to a collection concerning that war and its aftermath: a collection that merely continued the long tradition in the history of literature of writing about war, but, especially with the trench poets of World War I, a new beginning in poetry, a refutation of the Georgian aesthetic, an embrace of documentary realism, a moral aesthetic that transformed and continues to transform our understanding of the possibilities of poetry to this day despite enormous resistance to this perspective shift in our literary history, a literal shift from gazing up at skylarks to looking down at rats eating decomposing corpses and, concomitantly, this body of poetry was frequently characterized by a pugnacious rejection of staid cultural norms and the embrace of what may be called anti-poetry. I mention this because poetry that is seemingly concerned with sports, sports working as metaphor for the physical aspects of our being, meets that same level of ignorance, that dismissal of war poetry as an inferior sub-genre. Compounding the injury, in some of these pieces I have conjoined both war and sports, anathema to virtually everyone.

That young woman objecting to war as a subject of poetry merely evinced a cultural prejudice widely shared. But to have conformative poems about leaves changing color in the fall and dew on the grass, poems asking "How do I love thee?" (a poem recently taught at one of the military academies by people who mean well but do considerable harm when teaching poetry—not an uncommon occurrence) is disingenuous in a world that commands our attention be directed to the most pressing problems facing mankind: of course that runs smack into the most common prejudice of all: poetry and politics do not mix. Anyway such dismissals are rampant, even on my part as I bring certain rules of contemporary aesthetics to bear on my own work and that of others.

Definitions of poetry are profligate, often self-serving reflections of subjective prejudice, but assuredly poems that may be labelled sports poems or baseball poems or poems about athletic experience are certain to meet with considerable disdain by large numbers of readers and practitioners of the art of poetry. One objection to sports poetry is that it is the play of youth and we should grow up, turn our attention to matters of consequence, behave like adults but the problem, from the standpoint of intertextuality, is that previous poems, such as "Casey at the Bat," Marianne Moore's baseball poems, or a myriad of others, have defined the genre and prostituted it in much the same way as the movie *The Natural* bastardizes Malamud's novel. "Casey at the Bat," the poem usually cited to construct a derisive argument against sports poetry, has been defended by Donald Hall, perhaps because the nature of the game is about loss, loss so much more prevalent in baseball than winning, and loss has been a perennial theme in modern poetry. Both loss and error define the human experience; the best hitters fail 70% of the time compared to, for example, physicians who misdiagnose on average 20% of the time. A good poet barely bats .100. Probably why there is no Cooperstown for poets. Certainly, poetry changes over time, and what is acceptable or celebrated at one time is disparaged in another. Still, as Harold Bloom has written, poetry has the function to "defend the self against everything that might destroy it." Bad poetry destroys more than the self just as the narrow confines of aesthetic presupposition destroys poetry. More to the point, the primary responsibility of a poem is to take the tops of our heads off as Emily expressed it. Few sports poems have been capable of producing that effect, but that is true of most poems; the difficulty, the challenge is considerable. However, there is a surprising number that do.

When I was young, a student in one of Daniel Hoffman's creative writing classes, he said that the only unacceptable subject for poetry was poetry itself. He also said that if one couldn't handle rejection, this endeavor would be ill-considered. But the overriding antipathies towards poetry and politics, poetry and sports, poetry in narrative form, poetry that is not politically correct, poetry that is comprehensible and accessible, poetry that does not treat language as a divine instrument illuminating the cosmos—and the list goes on—largely defines this art form. That early lesson I was given simply means you can write about anything but don't expect much receptivity for it.

My defense, the quote of Wallace Stevens at the beginning of Part I of this collection, the idea that not living in the physical world is a sacrilege, is not considered a credible defense. It is easily rebuffed by the common belief that poetry is a cerebral celebration of the celestial. Fine. I admit the argument. But I also wish to offer a reminder of the joy of language embraced when young, a remonstration to the strong cultural prejudice that poetry by its very nature is child's play, something to be relegated to the grade school playground either with jump rope rhymes or "greasy, grimy gopher guts," a child's slap in the face of matronly, knuckle-rapping upholders of traditional societal values that infuse the academic world at every level. Poetry about sports, using athletic endeavors as a means of engaging the world, is actively discouraged by naïve, unschooled teachers and professors of English.

That bad sports poetry proliferates is a given, although such can be said of so many other sub-genres of poetry, of all literature in fact. I imagine there is not one single poem that could not be dismissed if critically examined in light of any of the myriad of aesthetic antipathies that inform the literary arts. If wars (including the poetry wars) are won on the playing fields of Eton, then they would be won by such as Captain Wilfred Nevill (Jesus College of Cambridge) of the East Surrey Regiment who on the first day of the battle of the Somme went over the top dribbling a football across no man's land and was quickly cut down, killed by enemy fire, and martyred forever. Such a beautiful image of human stupidity captured in the poem by author or authors unknown celebrating Captain Nevill's heroics, the poem entitled "The Game," which begins as follows:

On through the hail of slaughter,

Where gallant comrades Fall,

Where blood is poured like water

They drive the trickling ball.

That this poem defines mediocre, banal poetry should be a given, but regrettably it does not. One can argue about its celebration, how it is reflective of a culture's understanding of its heroism, its historical sacrifices for the nation, but such arguments should be met with strong rebuttals. Apart from the poem's banalities, that nonsensical, romantic (in the worst possible sense) sentiment was impossible to hold as the Battle of the Somme forever changed the character of poetry in English. And that carries over to sports poetry as well. The romanticism is supplemented by a realistic understanding of sport, its intrinsic physical artistry.

Argue as you will, sports and culture are intertwined as Ken Burns recorded in his *Baseball* documentary series. Any flight across the country reveals the enormous geographical attention paid to sports. Baseball, now superseded by football, as our national pastime, reveals our cultural identity. Is not every red-blooded American embarrassed by the sport of cricket? Aversions, antipathies, dislikes, intolerances, hostilities, aesthetic judgments, and preconceptions abound and define the literary arts as they define other artistic endeavors. In some quarters the literary arts and sports are mutually exclusive categories. Many years ago, I had two baseball players in one of my freshman English classes, both pitchers. One went on to a distinguished career in the majors and the other almost made it, but a tryout with the Brewers revealed a fast ball a few mph too slow. This student/athlete wrote a remarkable essay that garnered him a prize when submitted at the end of the term to a panel of judges looking at the best student writing of the year. He did not attend the awards ceremony; he would have been ridiculed by his teammates much in the same way Jim Bouton was derided for writing his tell-all book. Opposing players shouted derisive comments when Bouton took the mound, calling him, "Shakespeare," an epithet about as derogatory as it gets.

If one visits The Rosenbach in Philadelphia, one may view the writing life of Marianne Moore along with artifacts significant in her life including baseball memorabilia. I recall (nearly fifty years ago now) the docent's celebration of Moore's preternatural fascination with baseball, not something to be dismissed or ridiculed by either the general public or literary scholars. But it was almost as if a poet with an interest in baseball, a woman who is an ardent fan, is such an anomaly, such a remarkable curiosity, that she belongs in Ripley's Believe It or Not Museum next to the Vampire Woman or the Human Pin Cushion. Her baseball poems seem elementarily simple, merely a fan's appreciation, as unsophisticated or one-dimensional as her war poems, which were properly eviscerated by Randall Jarrell, though there are those who disagree as is the case with virtually all literary matters; however, Jarrell was as right about her war poems as I am about her baseball poems. As a general rule the literary reputation of the poet allows for critical lapses in the attention paid to that renowned author's work. If I were to suggest that Donald Hall's baseball poems do not represent his finest work, more than likely someone would suggest I be boiled in oil for this sacrilege.

1919, a very good year for corruption, as were all the previous years in our history, year of the Black Sox scandal, and like so many Americans growing up in post-war America (although most accurately there has never been a post-war period in American history), I found it unfathomable that a foundation, a pillar, of American society, the unassailable institution of baseball (a game defined by its strict set of inviolable rules) could be corrupted. I found such perfidy incredulous and so much out of sync with the political and historical understandings that were confirmed in the classroom and celebrated on T.V. during all the years of my youthful existence. Years later, however, after a stint in the Army during the Vietnam War, I was pursuing graduate studies in American Civilization, an interdisciplinary program, and I wished to explore the con man in American literature and history, examining everything from the Crédit Mobilier scandal and the Gilded Age to Melville's *Confidence Man*, "The Man That Corrupted Hadleyburg," the society that corrupted Sister Carrie, and of course Gatsby. As part of my forays into *Gatsby*, I wanted to read Eliot Asinof's *Eight Men Out*, but it was out of print so I contacted several used book sellers in downtown Philly and was met with a high degree of disdain, my request an umbrage, an affront to the social order, a deturbation of the class and caste structure that makes America a beacon to the unholy masses. They only sold books of great intellectual or archaeological value.

So snobbery, good old-fashioned highbrow rejections of the opiate of the masses (baseball and other culturally defining activities) rendered my request such a rankling of the social order that I must be considered such a rube, such a gauche, unlettered representation of the race that I should return to Mayberry and pursue my lowbrow, knuckle dragging existence far removed from the Main Line.

Again, the literary prejudice abounds. The same cultural prejudice that obtains concerning poetry, essentially an exercise for eggheads, an intellectual exercise that does not speak to people of ordinary intelligence, obtains even more so with poetry that uses sports as metaphor, as a connection to the physical side of human existence, only this side of the prejudice is shared by those who stake a higher claim for poetry—establishing some exalted position far removed from the physicality, the joyous exuberance of the body as it moves fluidly through the plane of life's physical existence. This is mind/body dualism at its worst.

Poetry and sports are play but serious play, serious business as well. Play, skipping home from school, catching an uncatchable fly ball, are acts of joy and grace and exuberance as are intellectual accomplishments. Edgar Alan Poe insisted the writing of poetry required an extreme level of rationalism, mathematical in its complexity, yet this association is seldom noted by academics and others who find poetry, the higher calling, to be of lesser value. If a pitcher defines his work as art, it is not much different from the physical creations of a ballet dancer. Few admit the similarity.

Decoherence may be defined as a disconnect, a state of poetry in which the underlying subject of the poem is separate from the poem itself, thereby giving credence to the reader's presuppositions. The effect of the poem is diminished by its subtext or back story or vehicle employed to ride the poem to its closure. Metaphor defines poetry, and, as Hannah Arendt has noted, metaphor represents the highest level of cognition. The best sports poems employ metaphor as the mechanism by which the physical world is conjoined with the cerebral. Still, in so many instances, we go out of our way to embrace the disconnect. Consider how Eliot's *The Wasteland* is not engaged as a war poem, as if WWI were not the underlying foundation of what is found there.

An old biological definition of life involved movement and, in the realm of art, Marcel Duchamp wanted "frequency of movement" in his paintings and Francis Bacon said language is "form and movement," so movement almost defines us as a species, defines our artistic achievements. A stationary existence is almost lifeless. Did not Coleridge meander from one side of the garden walk to the other in his philosophical peregrinations recorded in his *Biographia Literaria*, and does this not then conjoin poetry and movement and life itself? Yes, I admit the biological definition is now rather outmoded, superseded by later explorations, but still it holds largely true of our species. Poetry using sports as subtext, as backstory, as physical engagement, as metaphor, celebrates our physical response to the world.

So the question remains: why is there such a strong aversion to poetry that employs sports as a metaphor? For reasons of space just one objection may be considered here. A feminist response has been that sports are male-dominated and reflective of an inherent male superiority (real or imagined) in the world of athletics and that world mimics the world at large. Women should therefore separate themselves from the sports-dominated world men have created in order to construct a world very different from the one we currently live in, a world deemphasizing the competitive nature of athletics in favor of some empathic interconnected social structures. However, another set of feminist criteria employing equality of the sexes would embrace a female soccer player's right to pull off her sweaty jersey on the playing field after a victorious game and similarly insist that equal economic resources be accorded to women's sports. The conflict is contradictory and compounded by the view that because sports are such a large part of the patriarchy, they should not be given serious attention in literature, literature a defining cultural construct and once again male-dominated in the traditional canons. In effect, feminist writers would reject sports poetry for much the same reason they would reject poetry with war as its subject. Certainly, the feminist bias looms large, aided even by poems written by women such as May Swenson with her "Analysis of Baseball," a celebratory and playful but one-dimensional poem. Women then are not divorced from the world, in some measure accepting our cultural emphasis on athletics, but sports are not to be taken so seriously that they overshadow other feminist concerns. In effect a measure of cultural distancing and a familiar acceptance are conjoined. I have had women castigate me for my poem "She Throws Like a Girl," not looking past the title, but I grew up when many women did throw like a girl because the overhand throw was not part of their physical training. Ishi, the last Yahi Indian, couldn't throw overhand either, despite his extraordinary athleticism as evidenced by the way he mastered the longbow. The overhand throw was not part of his cultural experience. I have no doubt that now (making adjustments for age) there are women who could strike me out on three pitches and they would have a great laugh doing so.

It would be curiously inhuman not to expect a high degree of resentment over the attention given to athletics, the comparatively high valuations accorded to sports over the devaluation of scholarship or cerebral pursuits. To have poetry conjoined with sports, with a celebratory life of pure physical enjoyment, even though sports are merely the metaphor employed by the poem seems a slap in the face harder than any slam into the boards of a hockey rink. A high school chess team's championship will never be venerated the way a football trophy will. But the wondrous joy of being attuned to the physicality of the world, the mirific nature of canoeing a quiet wilderness lake at dawn, the perfect strike of a squash ball hitting the corners just right as it careens off the wall, or: playing kick ball in third or fourth grade, the ball kicked far over my head as I ran back to the playground fence, my back to the ball, and I reached out to where the ball should be in its descent, and it landed perfectly in my outstretched hands. That same feeling of exuberant joy is identical to the writing of a good poem. We live in a multiverse of aesthetic imaginings, as multi-dimensional as string theory: if, on a recently discovered exoplanet, it has been found that the atmosphere rains molten iron, should not our poetry as well admit to every possibility? We are large; we contain multitudes.

THE STINGER
TABLE OF CONTENTS

PART II

PART I

The greatest poverty is not to live in a physical world.

—Wallace Stevens

THE STINGER

Momma's boy my stepfather said,
always running behind your mother's skirt.
We got along that way for years,
a tension, sharp as a hunting knife
between us. But when the pretense was down
we'd play catch, usually at evening, after supper
when the sun left a lengthening shadow
across the yard. He'd throw them soft,
at first, maybe a little spin, a curve
that I'd misread, maybe a throw to the side
I'd have to stretch for. I'd wing it back,
and when I threw one wide and low he missed it,
had to run across the flower bed to chase it down.
The next few were the same, same speed,
same placement, setting me up for the stinger—
a ball thrown sharper, harder, with movement
that made me think or guess in the deepening shadows
of the setting sun. I'd take them hard
in the webbing of my glove—the speed,
the force, pulling my glove back, pushing it
into my chest, sometimes close to my face.
Then harder, where I'd miss it with the web,
catch it in the pocket where it reddened
my hand, bruising the bone, the stinger showing me
throw after throw what he meant: *Momma's boy*
it said, burning my hand with each catch,
Momma's boy as the sky reddened like a welt.

RUNNING WITH A COYOTE

Maybe we're both out of shape—
long past dark, the nightly run
at the base of the Rocky Mountains.
I cut up a hill winding through
a new and exclusive subdivision,
only a few lights visible through the windows.
The coyote joins me by the school,
keeps pace, me on one side of the street
he on the other. I breathe a little harder
because of the hill; I tell myself it's simply
the elevation, 6,235 feet, but the coyote
doesn't slacken his pace. I push harder,
enjoying the company. He looks over
and I nod, the pace pushing me,
my lungs working hard, my arms pumping.
He veers off at the next intersection,
cuts across a vacant lot. I wish him
a pleasant and invigorating run,
a night of good hunting,
a joyful howl that wakes the neighborhood.

SIXTH GRADE BUCKETS

She takes the inbound pass
drives down the right hand side of the court
every time, always dribbling with her right hand
until everyone knows what she'll do—
every defensive player, every parent
sitting in the bleachers,
and I can't help but think
how many times I told her
Dribble with your other hand;
go down the left side, or into the center
mix it up a bit, fake 'em out once in a while
catch the defense off guard,
keep 'em guessing, but she doesn't, even in practice.
So, in a tournament when they're behind by two,
time running out, she does the same thing,
rides the right side until this big girl—
arms like a dancing bear—
moves across the court anticipating the pick
and stops my daughter cold.
The bear moves her long arms to prevent a pass,
leans over to tie up the ball,
but my daughter fakes to her right, moves left
shifting the ball to her left hand, catching the defender
flatfooted, going the wrong way, and in a move
so quick she surprises everyone, she drives to the hoop
and lays it up to tie the game.
They win it easy in overtime.
And on the way home where I've learned
not to say anything about the game,
not even a hint or the mildest suggestion about her play
she says, *When we get home how about*
we go out and shoot some hoops;
there's plenty of time before dark.
And I smile, thinking there's plenty of time,
even for me, to learn *this* game.

FIRST GLOVE

Sometimes you know
just by staring
at that wall of gloves
in a sporting goods store,
but when your hand slips inside
you feel the ball
drive deep into the pocket
and your body knows
nothing can escape,
no routine fly caught in the sun
not a hard two-hopper off
the infield baked hard as concrete
in an August heat wave,
not a line drive that tails away
looking for that open spot in the outfield,
the gap where it can roll
all the way for a double.

I still have my first glove, the one
I bought with money saved from a paper route—
a black glove when everyone had cowhide brown
and signed by Karl Spooner.
I smoothed Vaseline into the leather,
rubbed it for hours until the leather
softened, and the glove
formed to my hand; I pressed a ball
into its pocket and tied it tight,
let it stay for three days, three nights,
so the glove closed perfectly
around the ball, ready to trap anything
that came within range, no crease,
no hard, cracked leather

ever to get in the way, to irritate, to
take away the concentration, the confidence,
and that first season I remember how nothing
got past, no matter where it was hit,
foul balls so far foul
they'd have been high up in the stands,
if we had played on a diamond
with something more than a low rise of bleachers,
but those slicing fouls ended up in my mitt
as did a long fly that went over my head
as I ran back, and back farther
until I was under it
as the ball reached the apogee of its arc
and then floated down as I was still backing up,
over the edge of a hill, moving backwards
down the hill until the ball tracked into my glove,
and I fell head-over-heels down the rough slope
still holding on to the ball.

I can still see the arc of that long fly,
its descent slowed by time, the frequent replays
I recall every summer when it's time to play
and I pull on that glove.

It wasn't until many years later
that I checked out Spooner's career:
sure I'd known he was a hot pitcher,
a rookie sensation,
but I wore the autographed glove,
no need, as a young boy,
to know anything more.

I learned the real story—
how in two games he struck out
twenty-seven batters and, then, season over,
expectations higher than a vapor trail,
he'd wrecked his arm in spring training
and never really came back.
His last game, game six of the '55 Series,
and Skowron, behind in the count,
hit a dying quail 210 feet for a home run,
this, Spooner's last pitch, high and tight,
a waste pitch, and there it went,
the game, and Spooner's career.

He spent the next year in the minors,
had surgery in '57, and then he was out,
back home where he got a job refinishing floors.
As he said, in two years he'd gone
from the Dodgers to floors, but I still played
with that glove, and it still feels good,
the pocket still soft, and I remember the catches.
And I wonder how often Karl Spooner remembers
those twenty-seven K's, the masterful pitching
in two games that made him
the hottest pitcher for that brief season,
the promise so close, and then everything
beyond reach like a squib
that falls in, that has eyes, that has
destiny written all over it.

WATER WOLF

My daughter watches
intently as I gut the pike—
she hates this, says this is
the last one and she won't
eat any more, not
this one, not any other;
we can catch them,
but we must let them go . . .

When she casts a silver spoon
into the weeds, a pike slams it,
takes it deep, wraps itself around
and around a weed; she lifts
her rod as I paddle over, following
her line. I free it, cutting the thick
stalk as deep as I can reach
and lift the long narrow pike
into our canoe; the spoon, too deep
to free, cuts gullet and gill;
blood covers my hands, my pants,
thickens into clots, to a red so dark
it's almost black. My daughter frowns,
displeased with my inability to free
the lure. No options left,
I thread the wounded pike
on a stringer, and we paddle back to camp:
released, the injured fish would simply slip
deep beneath the waves,
to rest in gray, decaying silt . . .

I gut this one quickly—
she wants to know what
each organ is, what it does.
I tell her the best that I can,
sorting through glistening reds,
soft blues and pinks.
I feel sharp spiny bones—
unlike walleye or bass—
as I wash the fillets,
then clean and dry the knife
I've used since a young boy.

I tell her in Canada the fish is christened
Pickerel; in the States it's named Pike
or Northern Pike, and in our mythology
Pike is called Water Wolf: she likes that,
the proper fitting of name to beast.

I put entrails and the long,
narrow carapace of our pike
out on the rocks, wait for the one-legged
gull to come from afar, homing
in on the scent; I tell her
it is only just that it is so—
a Water Wolf must have struck from
beneath, severed the gull's leg
with one lunge, those sharp teeth
slicing through that slender, yellow leg,
the gull only partly dragged under,
its buoyant form bobbing back
in a spray of foam and blood,
its wings beating the waves until
it rose above the long shadow of pike.

See, I said, *maybe this was the one*
that tried to make lunch of that gull—
now it will live sustained
by this strange reversal of fortunes.

But she is nine, too old to buy such tales,
and she grows quiet with a knowledge that strikes deep,
that grabs hold and won't ever let go,
burning through her life
like evening sun
red upon the water.

SOFT HANDS

According to legend Gene Tunney soaked his hands in brine
to toughen them for a fight.   –Author's Note

Even a small cut burns
and the man winces,
a whistle of breath through his teeth:
his daily ritual, communion with blood sport
that is ticket to money and fame—
those lesser rewards, if heaven really mattered.
No one remembers the almost there,
the second best: his hands soak
as if this were bare knuckle
boxing, gloves of little use,
offering scant protection.

He remembers previous fights, how he fought
with a broken knuckle, how it almost
healed and then another fight broke it again . . .
his adversary knows he's nursing his right,
relying on a flurry of sharp left jabs:
the subterfuge flowers like a welt, forces him
to throw a hard, countering right:
his opponent, anticipating, lowers his head
deliberately, directly into the punch
to break that hand again—
the sharp sting ran up his arm
and shorted in his brain, as if all the nerves were fused.

In graduate school I studied American philosophy,
Pragmatism, the works of Charles Sanders Pierce,
and Pierce used the analogy, the metaphor, of a boxer
anticipating his opponent's next move,
a pragmatic response, intuitive,
a model for human behavior;
and still the education has yet to take hold,
as if I've soaked my brain in brine
over the years and nothing gets through.
I've yet to anticipate anything that matters—
love, marriage, war, political battles,
skirmishes no one ever wins.
In the middle of night I awake,
my hands clenched;
with a clever feint
I walk into the punch.

This is an anthropology of the hands:
the speed bag blurs in the weak light
of the gym; the heavy bag gives
and gives absorbing the hands' energy,
evidence of that mythical dark matter known
only by inference.

His skin cracks and cracks again,
salt digging deep and deeper with each soak,
a sacrament of immersion, penance
for the acquisition of knowledge
and what he knows is transformed
to muscular awareness with perfect equilibrium.

In the ring he measures his opponent,
as if sparingly adding salt to his meal—
his hands blur in the harshness of ring light,
as much percussive power
and precision as a jazz pianist,
explosive hand movement too quick to see.
I saw Cecil Taylor play in a Philadelphia church,
his hands striking the keys too fast to follow
in the altar light.

I play with a heavy bag in the basement;
when no one's around I hit it
in a brief expenditure of useless energy.
It is a pretend game like philosophy,
little damage measured in the context of loss:
Suck it up I hiss under my breath
and laugh—
the only lesson residing in my skull.

After the fight, the pugilist returns to a moment
of reflection, a monk's prayerful quietude:
when he lifts his hand to his mouth
unraveling the tape, what he tastes,
what stays on his tongue,
is the benediction, the triumph of salt.

RUNNING AT MIDNIGHT

With each stride, cinders crunch underfoot
and the only other sound is of some night bird
calling. With earth and air cooled late
I can run farther, faster, longer
on this old school track,
the last cinder track in the city.
My mind focuses on the inner ring
of the oval circumscribing the football field.
I stay tight to the inside
remembering everything my high school coach
taught me about running—I keep my hands loose;
my arms pump with a steady rhythm.
Finishing a hard mile, my legs heavy, my mouth
filled with cotton, I sprint around the last turn,
pour it on down the straight and walk it off.
A voice calls out, breaking the spell, *Good night for a run.*
I search through the dark for that voice,
find a young woman standing on her front lawn
across the street; I try to catch my breath
to tell her how much easier it is to run
at night, in August, and how I do this
almost every night in summer
when the heat of the day, whatever I have to do,
drains energy like an overloaded circuit.
She walks across the narrow street
while I put on my sweats under the goal posts; I listen
as she talks about the quiet time of late summer
nights when she comes out to watch
and listen to the stars. There is a note of longing
in her voice, anticipation in the still air
that tells me what she looks for.
I draw further back into the shadows

back from the street lamp that might show her
I'm too old to run like this, too old to tell her
what she wants to hear, but it's only small talk after all,
something I've never been good at.
I refrain from telling her the few things I know,
that I've learned circling the track
one run after another, night after night,
season after season. She stands there
between the goal posts and the cinders,
her hands in her pockets, searching for words.
I wish her well, and jog back
to whatever awaits, slowing perceptibly,
leaving her beneath the circling summer stars,
all of us learning to pace ourselves
as best we can, searching, calling,
running through our nights. Some of the answers
swirl like insects around a street lamp,
some of them flare to ash in the light.

VACATIONS IN NORTHERN WISCONSIN, 1940's

My father fished for muskie,
my mother read novels on the shore
basking in the shadow of her hat,
bright ribbons streaming across the brim.
The long cast of a silver spoon
fluttered into the weeds as he felt
the sharp strike, the downward pull
of that mythical fish,
fought it for nearly an hour
until, played out, the muskie shone golden
when hauled over the wooden gunnels.
My father admired its beauty,
its great strength as it lay
gasping on the bottom of the boat,
gills heaving redder than the eye of the sun.
The muskie caught a second wind
sooner than my father, thrashed thunderously,
sent tackle and gear flying,
tangled its sharp teeth
in the net, and so my father sat on it,
held it down and yelled for help,
his cry echoing like the call of a loon across the lake.
My mom called Tony, owner of the resort,
who motored out to tow my father in
for photographs–my father, mother, muskie–
the life, the love, before I was born,
a story my mother told often
until she died, suddenly, last summer.
And yet the story holds on,
pulls me even deeper
than that mythical fish,

repeated with each loss like so many muskie,
legendary creatures long as a boat,
who would take your arm off
if you let it drag in the water,
the ones no one has ever caught,
or raised to the bright sun,
that crystalline light
dancing like lovers on the water.

44

The first time I saw Henry Aaron bat
he hit an easy pop up,
and I sat back, dejected, impatient,
waiting for his next chance at the plate.
It seemed forever—I was only eight,
had time only for winning,
the grand moment, heroic gesture—

Always the last of the ninth,
2 out, behind by 3, bases loaded,
3 and 2 the count—seventh game of the World Series,
and I had Henry Aaron's power;
I would foul off the next, a curve low and outside
just nicking the corner, staying alive
as the world waited, balanced on the outcome
of the next pitch.

Always it hung across the plate,
belt high, as my wrists broke,
and the hard crack of the ball
resounding off that bat rose above the world,
beyond the deep left center of everything.

A thousand times, hit always to the same place
deep in the stands, the place I watched
waiting for Aaron's next turn at the plate.

And again he was out and again—
I could not understand
how anyone that good could fail;
I could not know the best fail most the time.

The next game went the same
until the eighth and Aaron
took a strike—a ball—
then swung and missed—the next
was low—count even
the sign shook off and
Aaron guessed it right,
picked up the rotation of the seams,
knew it as his body sprung, forearms extended,
wrists breaking, unleashing the coiled
power in his bat,
cleats twisting into the dirt:

Trajectory of a bullet, sharp rise
above the plane, the fall—
he noted where it hit
and rounded first, head down,
the noise we made like the voice of God
thundering in the great man's ears.

I didn't want the cheers to stop,
the next batter to come up to the plate
congratulating Henry with a slap
on his outstretched hand.
I wanted him to run the bases endlessly
never reaching home
as I struck out, as I popped up
going from game to game
playing far into the night,
far into the years.

AUBADE

It is cool in this room
oblique to the sun
and still early—
early enough to push the sheets away
and lie in the cool breeze
transforming morning shadows
into carousels of light;
pale curtains billow up
to ceiling heights
and then descend
like parachutes of dandelion seed.
Your shoulders shiver at the touch.

The fan, on all night, stutters and skips.

If I were a boy again
it would be time for baseball
or flying model airplanes
or the hunting of birds;
those years of play have not been lost,
still course like blood through every thought—
I hunt the signs that you will stay
and not get dressed, or move about
simply to be up and doing what needs be done:
wait, until the sun is overhead,
until the insects sing with hate,
until a ball drives through that plate of glass.

SLEDDING WITH KERRY
for my daughter, age 8

There's too much drag
on the runners of this sled
and the saucer, too, stops short.
We barely get to the bottom
when we're abruptly stopped—
this snow heavy and deep.
Again, we trudge back up the hill
and dream of a faster ride.

She thinks of it first, the half
sheet of veneered paneling, slick
as a film of oil on water,
and we try it, holding on
to the fence at the top of the hill—
I ask, *Are you ready?*

When she says *yes*, I let go, and we fly—
clouds of fluffy snow explode
in our faces as we spin
between trees, too fast
to hold on and we roll off
airborne into a sea of snow—
she laughs, crystal ornaments of ice
catch the light in her hair,
snow deep down in our boots,
up our sleeves, like magic
all my years disappear
like the cold melting down my back.

A THEOLOGY OF CIRCUMNAVIGATION

Mastery is one thing: reverence another,
souls redeemed one at a time.
A well placed single seldom receives
the accolades of a ball knocked out of the park,
out of play actually, out of bounds.
I imagine somewhere a Zen master
preaching the virtues of the single,
a well hit ball between an array
of fielders, nothing to get excited about,
merely a man on first, an imperceptible threat,
but two more and a run crosses the plate.
This is the parable of a man without power,
nibbling away one hit at a time,
a lesson that transcends the hobbling of time.
The master sits cross-legged, bat across
his knees, waiting in the aura of the on-deck circle.

IN NORTHERN ONTARIO,

On the banks of a sandy lake,
an old snapping turtle basks in the sun
far out of reach of the warm, pulsing water.
Two leeches suck on the opened flesh of his stubby neck
making it hard for his head to retract.
I take my knife still stained with the blood
of pickerel and bass and cut them from his heavy dark green
and brown flesh— they splatter thick blood
when I smash them stone against stone.

I search for more.
His ridged triangular plates recall
the armor of a stegosaurus, the instincts
of fifty million generations. Patiently
his black obsidian eyes follow me
as I find heaped rings of parasites,
like a nest of baby snakes, clinging
to the leathery folds of his webbed feet.
I cut them like bloody worms, but timorously,
as I recall baiting a snapper with a stick
as a young boy, fascinated by his ancient power
to break it in two.

Primitive surgery done, the pale pink ooze
will cure in the sun, wash clear in the lake.
I feed him entrails from fish, launch the canoe
to catch us some more.

How sweet the lakewater tastes over fallen tangled
trees clearly seen in depths far out from shore, and yet
some of the bass have round yellow worms, some
almost orange, curled in the sweet translucent
flesh throughout the caudal peduncle, between
the neural spines. I crush the ones I can find
after digging them out or burn them,
in the fire, along with the heads of pike
and sunfish—their gills still open and close,
their eyes still follow movements of my hand
as orange flames feed on them
with their sharp teeth.

No sign of the turtle when I return—
the scarred snapper has slipped off,
his heavy shell warmed like a stone
in the afternoon sun—
not even a break in the water
as far as the eye can see
or the light can reach.

OLD GUYS PLAYING HOOPS

Weekday noons at the Y
they meet for a workday break
to keep in shape,
practice a few lay-ups,
a few set shots, until
they're ready for a game—3 on 3,
gray in their beards, a roll of fat
around the middle,
wearing the same shirts
they wore in high school,
with the same low numbers,
number 3, or number 6,
from a time long before
00, a time when Bob Cousy
was the great ball handler,
a time before slam dunks
which the sign on the backboard says
aren't allowed anyhow.
And the shots don't fall
as often as they once did,
and the quickness around the pick
isn't there the way it used to be
and they bend over at the waist
catching their breath
more often than they used to.
But when the hard pass on the break

catches the defender a bit slow
and off guard, and the ball lifts
off the old forward's fingers,
rises sweetly above the rim,
slides through the net
with the smoothness
of a magician's bullet through silk,
he forgets the bandage
wrapped around his knee, and remembers
tournament shots he made in high school,
the dance after the big game, the girl
on his arm, the long kiss at the door—
a time when nearly everything
fell as perfectly as a fall away jump shot
or his hand along her silken waist.

BEYOND THE HAGGIS TOSS

All these sports I've never heard of,
never played, flinging the geavelick,
for example, never tossed it, never will. So when
I'm in Budapest, late one night, walked-out tired,
I turn on the TV, flip through channel after channel,
looking for CNN, in English,
and I find instead a channel presenting a sport
unusual in its appreciation of the aesthetic
moment, that moment in sports when the intellect,
the body, work with such perfect synchronicity
that reverence, prayer, the eternal faith of
the hopeful athlete, the committed fan, is drawn
contemplatively to the pleasure
of a perfect toss, analogous to Reggie
Jackson's sanctifying throw from right field
to third base, so perfect in its arc, its velocity,
its accuracy, that the runner was out with what
he said was a lucky shot, a one time throw,
and given the chance he'd try for third again;
to which Reggie responded, *Well then,*
I'll just throw him out, again. It is that
perfection I find as a dart flies
to the center of all things, not of the
dartboard merely, but of everything,
as in the theory of everything, this throw
effects a perfect balance, perfect
synchronous movement—the dart
leaves her hand and her right breast

moves harmonically with the throw. This
is topless darts, a sport I am
immediately drawn to, the circumference
of the eye, breast, circles of the dartboard, all
concentric in their movement—rippling
from that perfect center, circumference theory
superintending the physics of aesthetic
contemplation—woman against woman,
each steps to the line, throwing three,
retrieving her weapons as the other awaits
to set at the line—Always, with a right handed throw,
the right breast moves in perfect symmetry—
a weaponeer's realization that arm and
armament are one. It is a pleasant contemplation,
devoid of the politics of sport:
if there were a world series of topless darts
I would not live or die with the outcome—
blessed by an aesthetic epiphany, the perfect throw
of enlightenment, lovely in this moment
of pure Euclidian delight.

WHAT NOBODY LEARNS

In history class the athlete
who letters in three sports
dreams—even on game day—
of practice, of how energy
contained in the classroom
all day long
explodes on the ball,
a perfect afternoon
when everything falls just right.
His teacher knows what has happened,
what will happen, based on the past.
That is the reason for studying,
for knowing, what has gone on before.
It is predictability within a circumscribed
time-frame, a certainty that mastery
of all that has gone on before
will give to the present
understanding a reluctance
to repeat ancestral error.
But the athlete, ignorant perhaps
even of those who have played
his game before, thinks only
of the moment, of time
focused on one shot, one play,
one well-timed hit. It is the arrest
of history, the creation of the moment
that makes history, which concerns him,
unknowing as he is, and the teacher
professes the past, the present arrested
in the stale air of the classroom.
The playing field awaits:
within limits of the historical
imagination a ball slams into the gap.

ALUMINUM

Whether it's baseball or golf I don't care,
I don't care if the ball goes farther
or tails away on a line drive,
don't care if it improves my game
or makes me a better person, life
and sport being one and the same:
at least that's what all the books say—
and the coaches—whether they've read one or not,
and I believe them, but I still don't care;
it's not the same: A driver with a head
the size of a gourd, a sweet spot
deeper than the sky—so what,
and those shiny metal bats that glint
in the sun on an afternoon perfect
for baseball—that rinky-dink ping
that sounds like someone dropped
an heirloom teacup on a rock—hell
I'd rather play Scrabble at the old folks
home than listen to the sound
of an aluminum bat hitting the ball—
When I die I want to remember the sweet sound
of a ball hit with wood, the sound God
made when he created darkness and light—
the sound of a tree a thousand years old
growing into the pitch, singing
all the way to the deep center of everything

THE BIGGER THEY ARE

I wrestled 112
though my natural weight
was 120 so it is easy to see
how ineffectual I would have been
at right tackle, football just not
in my genes. But I went out anyway,
and on one golden afternoon
our future quarterback, a big guy
even for a freshman, at least a head
taller, maybe 50, 60 lbs. heavier,
and fast for a guy his size,
fakes it and runs through the line
and I give chase, cutting off the angle
as he feints and cuts left, thighs pumping
hard and high as I catch him from behind
just when he thinks he's going all the way,
my arms close around his legs
in a diving tackle, picture-perfect,
pulling his legs to my chest
just like the coach had taught,
the way we dreamed it could happen.
He falls hard, bounces on the churned up
field in a cloud of chalk, chunks
of earth clinging to his face guard,
knuckles skinned, grass stains on his uniform.
We're both banged up, but the breath
of autumn fills my helmet, the scent
of afternoon sun, and the quarterback
oh so slow to get up from the punishing dirt.

LURE

It fools no one—
smooth wood
camouflaged
green and brown
like a minnow
or small perch—
a line of silvery glitter
along the gills,
its red eye
artificial,
(a blind man would be ashamed):
its underbelly
gray as the underside
of a stealth bomber or B-52,
and there is no disguising
the lethality
of its treble hooks;
they twist seductively
on a slow retrieve.
One wonders how anything
could be fooled—
fish or fisherman
it doesn't matter.
On a hot summer night
preparing for the next day's
hunt for musky and pike,
I sharpen the piercing barbs,
lift the plug to the light,
admire row upon row
of teeth marks
sunk deep in the wood.

THE QUARRY

No Trespassing signs
aren't much of a deterrent
when you're seventeen
and the water is the deepest
blue-green you've ever seen—
promise of cool water
after dark, a forbidden swim
into unmarked dangers,
no line of floats, no lifeguard,
just the quiet call of crickets
and a few stars charting a safer course.
It is a tradition taking off our clothes,
diving in, swimming to the rock ledge
across the quarry where we could rest,
catching our breath, stilling the heart
to tell stories, brag of girlfriends,
pronounce our futures, rag on
teachers for their silly rules.

And on that night, late,
when even our friends were fast asleep,
almost on a dare you and I
parked down the road,
snuck over the fence,
walked to the water
to watch the still moon float.
My arm around your shoulders
slipped to your waist, a touch
among the crickets, night birds calling,
quarry stone still warm
from the lengthening sun.
The moon rode on the silken water

as we kissed, as we broke
apart to feel the embarrassed thrill
of being nude. We jumped in,
the water deep and cool as a kiss,
the touch of your wet arms, your back,
treading the deep soul of the night.
And we swam, breaking the moon
into small pieces of light and water,
and when we crawled back out
your arms shivered, your shoulders,
as much from my kiss as from
the late night chill.

What could have happened
in all these years
to break that spell, to lose everything
the water dreamed?

POPPING UP TO SECOND

A good eye
isn't good enough
when the pitch burns
across the plate
hotter than you've ever seen it
before, but hitting is simply
a matter of adjustment,
as all things become simply
matters of adjustment,
the exchange of one value for another:
one marriage, one house, one job,
one school, easily exchanged
with a simple shift
from one stance or position
to some other, often but a minor variant
of the one before. So, maybe, this is the first
lesson, on a field packed hard
and worn by children
playing ball before the bell rings,
playing again during recess and after school
until it's time to go and play
the game of family and homework.

But one doesn't know any of this
under a sun so bright
it burns past middle age
past demolition of the old school
and the playground now the site
of a new one made of concrete block
and a metal roof—rather like a prison—
the architecture of schools and prisons
being one and the same.

Still this was a game that mattered
being in second place
in the grade school league
and the pitcher, rumored to be faster
than any we'd faced before, could seal up first
with a win. So I dig in,
concentrate, and swing hard
at the next pitch right down the middle,
but I'm too fast, ahead of the ball
as it lifts lazily into the sun
backing up the second baseman
who puts it away for an easy out.

When I die I want all my adjustments—
so right at the time—to come into play;
I'll have the perfect wife, a perfect child,
a car that never breaks down, a house
that never needs any repair or restoration,
and a job where people at the top
actually like what I do. I'll hit
a liner so hard the pitcher flattens
on the mound, and the ball will scream
past the second baseman
who won't even see it or hear it
until it takes off his ear,
and I'll waltz into second
and just stand there
in the diamond's studious glare
adjusting my eyes to the sun
burning the world to perfection.

THE HARD SLOW DANCE OF THE PUGILIST

A flurry of punches
none doing any damage
the boxers grin at each other

mouthpiece exposed like a death mask
another series of punches, body blows
uppercuts, a safe break

they dance the way lovers dance
in that first competitive embrace
feeling each other out

finding the point of vulnerability
the weakness ripe for exploitation
a hard right followed by a sequence

of jabs, mathematical in their precision
like harmonic chords
strung across the universe

only in this case the limits are the ring
and there's no escaping
the hard slow dance

as they embrace, holding on
in the late rounds like lovers
who have nowhere else to go

INDIAN SUMMER GRASSHOPPERS

Today, on the bike trail,
a flight of grasshoppers
stretches for miles; one after another
flicks into the air, wing-flash
veering from my predatory bike.

It is the sun that brings them
to the tarmac, heat stored
in the black trail, a gentle grade
where once freight trains moved
from town to town, old depots
torn down like wooden bridges,
trestles coated with tar.

Once, in tenth grade,
for a biology class assignment,
we hunted them unmercifully,
pinned them to a cardboard mat,
labeled them and got our A's.

Now, I swerve to miss them,
preferring to watch them rise
and sing, a breath of autumn
riding on their wings.

SAY HEY!

The afternoon I saw Willie Mays
stumble in center field
coming in for a looping fly,
the world didn't change
perceptibly, the earth
wobbled no more than usual
in its orbit, all the colors
of summer were the same.

When I was young
I practiced shagging flies
summer after summer
catching them like Willie Mays,
close to the chest,
imitating his famous basket catch.

I'd throw a scuffed ball against
the schoolhouse wall, against the side
of a neighbor's garage, catching the ball
as it bounced high overhead
arcing into my glove—
with one quick and fluid release
I'd throw to third, nailing the runner
as he slid hard into the tag.
He was almost always out—I never cheated:
if the ball stuck in my glove for an instant,
if I missed the target by inches,

I'd throw it again and again, a hundred times,
even in a summer rain,
long past dinner, past the angry voices of parents
calling and calling for me to stop,
to put the glove down and come home.

That day, watching Willie Mays,
his misplay stinging like a foul tip off the hands,
I tried to recall those afternoons
spent roaming the outfield
catching line drives
and shagging flies over my shoulder,
recollection aching like an old injury—
the deep muscle hurt that never goes away.
I remembered reading how old ballplayers
seldom come back to the park, leaving the game
to younger players, many of whom
don't know the history, the records,
the names of great players
from even a generation ago. And yet
on long summer afternoons,
outfield grass smelling like clover
even in the dead of winter,
the dead space late at night,
I still catch the ball close to my chest,
still make that long throw from center
with a beautiful and terrible accuracy
nailing the runner for the last out.

But the last out is never
the last out—the jaunt back
to the infield is never replayed—
always I am standing there
waiting for the next pitch,
leaning a bit, anticipating,
given the predisposition
of the batter, given the pitch I know
is coming, given that time
is suspended
like the sun, overhead,
the ball just an endless
summer from my mitt.

BODY BLOWS AND HEAD SLAPS

After the bell, Friday Night Fights
Look sharp, feel sharp, be sharp
played out like a fighter repeating

the same sequence of hits—
right cross to the jaw, left jab
jab, jab, jab

uppercut: the mantra rang in our ears
with the same repetitive flail
body blow after blow

fist meeting fist, a parry
a hard clench on the ropes
the break, a cut targeted, hit,

hit again with a hard twist
opening the cut wider
until blood burns in the boxer's eye

gloves covered with blood
spots of blood on the canvas
as again the bell rang

Look sharp, feel sharp, be sharp
and we *were*, gloriously
with the courage of boys pretending

beaming, as we took off our shirts
moved furniture in the living room
careful of lamps, collectibles

bric-a-brac, and we were at it
no gloves, just the flat of our hands
for those blows to the face

a slap to the head careened off my temple
no matter how much protection
my left hand gave

always a punch riveted through, always
a stinging and bloody nose, my bell rung
and the metaphor held true

I cringed at the hard head slap
teaching me what I'd always known
that I hate getting hit in the head

and no defense I worked on ever worked
against a fast flurry of fists
because the rules never worked either

the hard hand closed
in the seriousness of battle
red welts and bruises lasting for days

I grew up burning to get close, to get even
for every loss, every wrong, to tie everyone up,
back all opposition against the ropes

a body punch out of the clinch
stopping that hard right, that irritating jab,
my snaking left out of nowhere

slamming its way home,
all justice and mercy
in the sweet pleasure of my fist

from THE ADCOCK POEMS:
FRED HANEY MISMANAGES HISTORY

Always, someone screwed up
your stats—one bonehead play,
one misadventure, after another.
And these were the good guys,
great players, hall of famers,
who must remember even better
than the rest of us how you destroyed
that perfect game pitched by Harvey Haddix,
twelve perfect innings, when perfection
just wasn't perfect enough. You belted a home run
with two on in the thirteenth,
but Henry Aaron ran off the base path
thinking the game over as Mantilla crossed
the plate, so you passed up Aaron
rounding second, and you were out—
one less home run, two fewer ribbies,
and just a ground rule double
to show for it all.

But errors are just part of the game:
Yet again against the Giants
a grand slam, an RBI single
and you at the plate crushing
another ball into the bleachers
what should have been your second
grand slam of the day, except,
on the play before,
Mathews had inexplicably broken
for third leaving Bruton with no choice
but to head for home, dead as any
game bird you hunted in Coushatta,

Louisiana—and worse, with four hits
in four at bats, a single, a double, two
home runs, two runs scored, eight driven in,
Haney, noting your slump no doubt,
pulls you for Frank Torre, thus
depriving you of another chance,
another record, Haney not caring
in the least about the creation of history.

A game of inches we're told,
and everyone makes mistakes—
history just one blunder after another
and then the excuses: All those memoirs,
all that time, to rectify a willful ignorance,
one error, one excuse, following another.

Gods don't make excuses, don't ghost write
their memoirs, and baseball is a lesson of mercy,
of being at the mercy of others, at the mercy
of one's own misadventures, one's own
miscalculations.

If you hadn't dug in
just daring pitchers to brush you back,
if you could have just pulled the ball,
even a little, if there weren't all those pitches
recorded as broken bones season after season . . .

Still, no one ever had a day like yours—
four home runs, almost a fifth, just inches
from the top of the wall—a double—
and the record still stands: Eighteen total bases.
When Alzheimer's took your mind out of the game
I trust your body dug in at the plate,
and with the bases loaded, you went out
swinging for the fences

WINTER NUDES

In January's coldest light
a flock of starlings
crosses the window,
their shadowy flight
races across your cheek
like memory
like the time years ago
when child play filled the morning
drowning the gray skies of winter,
when I yelped at your playful bite
as we wrestled, as I pinned you,
your arms pressed back,
your breasts pushed up
waiting for the attack
of my tickling beard, and I,
in my counter-move,
as your teeth sunk deep
into my shoulder, kicked out
the window by the bed, escaping
from the unfairness of your teeth,
and the cold air rushed in
like laughter filling the room,
a deep breath, the sharp sting
of love and broken glass.

SHE THROWS LIKE A GIRL

She keeps the bat off her shoulder,
concentrates on the pitch,
waits, measures its speed,
isn't fooled by any fakery
in my windup, nails it,
drives it hard over the neighbor's fence—
and I'm happy as any father
can be: She has a good eye,
loves the feel of making contact,
the sound, the resonant movement
of the world driven deep.

When we play catch she lacks control,
especially when she wings it,
trying to put some real speed on the ball;
she's just like her father, and the reason
I played right—good catch, lousy throw
to second or third. So I wonder how
she'll do in a game, but when the ball
jams into the gap, she runs it down,
whirls, takes a step and throws it—
a sharp, hard liner that goes back
the same way it came out, and the girl
playing second doesn't have to move
the target of her glove; she tags the runner
for an easy out: And I think
how my daughter throws like a girl—
my girl—with an arm like spring steel.

PART II

We made too many wrong mistakes.

—Yogi Berra

INNER CITY BASKETBALL

He has little chance of going pro
though an excellent scorer, made the all-state
team twice, but his grades were poor
so he ends up not getting a scholarship
and finds his way to my class,
a community college English course,
English for dummies, English as a second
language for those who never learned a first one.

Towards the middle of the semester
when my car breaks down in the suburbs,
I walk back from the garage where my car's been towed,
walk because buses are deplorable
and dangerous, fighting on every other run,
petty thievery, kids on drugs: I remember once
sitting across from a young man
with eyes a brilliant blue, pupils pinpointed,
the blue concentrated with a terrible beauty
by the drugs. I walk through neighborhoods
one had better not be caught in at night,
though daytime isn't that much safer.

Halfway back I hear a voice calling
my name so I turn, look across a schoolyard
and see my student throwing buckets.
I stop, walk over, and we talk. He tells me
his story, how he could have gone to Penn State
if his grades were better, how he has to get
at least a 2.5 before he's allowed to reapply.
He tosses me the ball; I look up
at the rusted rim, chain for a net, and shoot—

a simple set shot—it bounces on the rim and rolls
harmlessly into his hands: he steps back, dribbles
and shoots from beyond the key. I watch
the ball arc across the inner city sky
into the net, chain noise rebounding across
the playground. We talk some more,
and then I have to leave, the day
working its way towards evening,
sun sinking over an endless line of row houses,
the run-down school, its windows barred or bricked.
I wish him well. As I walk on I can hear
his ball dribbled on the asphalt, carom off the backboard,
imagine it sliding through the net.

.   .   .

At the end of the term I've corrected
everything I can; it's up to him.
His last paper is borderline, between B and C.
I think the game is his only way out—
and mine—both of us stuck in a hellish place.
I give him an A, his ball echoing through the chains.

SWIMMING TO THE ISLAND

It looks close enough
as the lake quiets, water smooth
in the moonlight, but distance
is deceptive, in the water, in exultant youth,
the refractions of both.
Half way across, strokes easy and strong,
the narrow beach seems no closer,
no nearer, than the young girls
who bathed there in the weekend sun.

He stops, gulps air, treads water,
floats on his back, noting constellations
swimming across the sky. The lake, spring fed,
pockets of warm and cold water, moves
with his movement, offering a natural resistance,
the hold of air and water, muscle and heart.

Another flurry through the alternating springs,
and he stops again, floats easily, turns over
on his back, moving his arms as if making
snow angels in the water: a falling star
burns, tracking a downward glide,
expires in the black waters above.

He turns face down, kicking, conscious
of the flutter, the engine propelling him,
his arms tight to his side, torpedo-like,
his head under the surface
tunneling through chambers of water.
He looks down into the dark cavern
of the lake, his eyes open for the first time,
knowing the water was without light,

the depth closed to any perception,
but some finny thing moved below, sinuous,
scaled, water pumping through cetaceous gills.

His head lifts; his mouth swallows air,
water, his eyes note the black tree line ahead—
silhouette of the island like some prehistoric
beast, quiet, feeding in the nightly waters,
ancestor, perhaps, of creatures that devoured
whole civilizations, who fought with the gods.

He puts his head down, works his arms
furiously for a moment, takes another gulp of air,
kicks hard, expends all that pent up kinetic energy;
his muscle burns with the overload—he stops,
sunk in exhaustion, worries about the beast's disappearance,
the moon occluded by venomous clouds,
thinks of resurrection as washed up bait.

Closer, perhaps in water shallow enough
to stand, sand bars often extending
past the point, washed away in storms, rebuilt
in the wash of waves against the bar,
and so he stood, sinking,
the bottom no nearer than before:
he lets himself sink, vertically,
resting in the cool wash, scrotum hard,
penis shrunk, fingertips shriveled, lungs tight,
kicks upward like perch leaping
above the surface as a pike strikes from below,
breaks into the medium of night,
frog-kicks and pauses, kicks
and pauses, and tries again, sinking
down until the touch of weeds

tells him he is close—he kicks hard,
drawing his arms back, thrusting forward,
the reach of sand within his grasp.

He crawls out, lies gasping on his back.

A myriad of stars, like luminescent fish,
swim across the night:
his restful breath returns.
Always he saw himself in water
accepting its grace, its giving,
and never a careless thought to going back
to what appears beyond his grasp
as if clenching his fist
on a handful of water.

                    Boundary Waters, 1966

WORLD SERIES, 1968, SOUTHEAST ASIA

On the other side of the world
it don't mean nothin'—
the slow tedium of the pitcher
holding the ball in both hands
rubbing the seams as if a talisman
that could save his life,
and, if the charm didn't work,
to lose it, just another game lost
in the box scores, a minor loss
buried in history; and the batter
tries to stay alive waiting for that one pitch
knowing there's a wicked one out there,
a bullet that has his number on it.

Men lose their gods at a time like this,
embrace the unthinkable, that gods die,
that men can kill them—1,2,3—just like that.
It's never the same.

I turn away from the monotone
of the TV in the Officers Club,
the game just background for the war,
order another scotch and soda,
await the quiet ambush of that sweet drink
mixing the dream of Asia, new gods
charged with destruction
destroying the old gods, because, why not?
And losing it all doesn't matter
as the game dies like the loss of a friend
one has no time to mourn and that so easy anyway
in a game where deaths are recorded like outs
and neither the dead nor the living keep score.

Nothing moves in the heat, the alcohol stupor,
the wait. Lying back in the hootch
I watch geckoes cling to the ceiling,
the only friends I trust now as I study,
dispassionately, the gods carving themselves
into pieces, and one of them turns and says,
Who's next? What about you? and laughs.

On the playground the ball
wants to be hit, to make everyone move
in the summer stillness, sunlight
curving through space
folding a fly ball into the deep
field of sky, then falling back, under it,
waiting, watching the beautiful arc,
the beautiful white of the ball
against the beautiful blue of a cloudless summer.

This is no dream for a soldier
in times like these: no routine fly,
no line drive hit hard, right to the center
of his chest so he doesn't have to move
even a single step
as the ball slams into his glove
with the sound and feel
that everything makes sense.

On the long flight back, the perfect geometry
of playing fields shows certainly through the clouds,
the bases white as always, outfields still green
but so far away they're not worth coming home to,
not worth what it takes to get back.

To know this before returning
is the game one has to play,
the hard won price of admission,
the accords one can never live up to.
It could have been Gibson on the mound
who held the ball too long, could have been
Cash or Kaline who stepped out of the batter's box—
Whatever, it doesn't matter, the game slowed
past all time that matters in this world.

GARAGE DAY

Cleaning out his cluttered garage
he finds an old fielder's mitt,
leather cracked and stiff after years lost
in the accumulated debris of minor triumphs,
minor defeats, accumulations of little consequence
passing from one interest to the next,
passing time, as he used to, throwing baseballs,
tennis balls, even golf balls, at odd angles
bouncing them off garage walls, the roof,
impossible caroms out of corners
that he deftly caught or came close to,
making spectacular catches, the energy
of the ball, its wicked spin, caught deep
in the glove, tamed like nothing else since.
He tosses a ball in the air, catches it, throws,
catches it again and again, takes a hard
grounder off the garage door,
a wicked hop to the chest, throws—
catches— throws, in ritual familiar as a sacrament
until crickets sing in the shadows,
until the sky softens like his glove to evening.

THE JOY LINED OUT

> Roger Maris hit 60 home runs
> in fewer at bats than Babe Ruth

Wearing the unmistakable crewcut
of a ballplayer of his time, late fifties,
early sixties, and still looking
like every baseball card they'd ever
made of him, he gets turned away
at a reception in his honor, and to honor
other players who had made their marks,
and you wonder how any security guard
could have made *that* mistake, even
in a world filled with one blundering error
after another. So he takes his family
upstairs to dine alone, the applause,
the recognition still not there
for him to hear, and any accolades
in the papers are just a simple
rectification of bad press, recognition
of ignorance, a mean-spirited ignorance
that reached all the way to the top.
And in the films of his accomplishments
they still call him *surly* and *taciturn*,
as if to diminish his talent
with charges of temperamental character,
assassination in the press that leaves
any young boy or historian of the game
with a bitter taste in his mouth
like blood from a bad hop on a hard infield
where the lip is cut deep against the teeth.
And I can still taste the blood
when I see pictures of him smiling,

playing to the fans in right field,
the joy in his face on those baseball cards
reflecting that perfect enjoyment
we all knew growing up playing ball
in the backyard or on grade school diamonds.
It is the smile of a man who knows he can hit,
who can feel in his bat the long ball carrying deep
beyond any reasoned measure of his game.

CANOE TRIP

I scouted rapids
from a ridgeline above the river:
swirling water turbid, dark,
river banks crumbling, undercut
with this swollen rush from heavy rain.

On my left was a farmer's field,
plowed under, ready for spring planting.
Looking down at the water
I didn't notice the pit
until I was almost at its edge.
It was filled with dead pigs,
a few young ones, the rest mostly fetal
with umbilical cords still attached—
dozens of them heaped over a few large, gray sheep,
a couple of rats, a muskrat
poised, swimming through all that death,
its head resting on the back of a pig.
It looked almost alive swimming there
except its eyes had been plucked by the birds.

I was upwind as I stood at the edge
watching rain pelt down
on small pink bodies heaped several feet high.
Edging back, I skirted around
to the left, walked down along the ridge
on the other side of the pit;
its stench gagged me, and I choked . . .

The dead were on the wire,
sprawled outside the perimeter,
with many more along the tree line;
a few were inside where they'd overrun
a fire team on the left.

In the sun their bodies started
to swell—parts of bodies hung
in the trees, one arm swinging
like a Mexican piñata.

We searched most of the bodies, but the smell
made nearly everyone throw up—
and two were booby trapped.
The week before one had played possum,
and a man was killed next morning
when he came out to search through the dead.

Their stench gagged deep in our lungs,
and defenses were so torn up, engineers
just came and bulldozed all those bodies
together in a pile and buried them
under a few feet of earth—
one arm and part of its hand stuck up,
almost waving good-bye,
before it too was plowed under . . .

I walked back, past a woodchuck
hanging in a tree
wedged in the V of some branches—
a farmer's lethal warning—
felt the rain
stinging my eyes.

I put in maybe thirty yards downstream
from where I'd landed—
decided to take my chances
with the rocks.

A FIND IN THE WOODS

In moss and wet leaves,
fur and bone scattered
in a tethered trail of sinew
and cartilage, I unsheathe
my knife, sever the grinning
head at the third vertebra
and hold it in my hand
admiring the distant look
in its eyes, the bright teeth,
the smooth mandible of delight.

Returned home, I put a bucket of bleach-
water out back, toss in the skull
and wait, three days, four:
a frothy cream rises
to the surface; I skim off the lace
of hair, bits of floating meat,
and watch the bone turn white
and whiter as days pass.

When it is clean and pure
as bleached light, I hold it again,
replace missing teeth
that have come loose, scattered
on the milky bottom of the pail.
I lift it to the sun and see myself grinning
from the smooth architecture
of a past I can't help but feel
in dark and bloody marrow
that begs to race through a late
chill of evening, chasing
along freshly spotted blood trail
whatever it is I will come to
in scattered remains I leave behind.

THE LAKE

On this return
he found lake water
darker than before, as if the water
were laced with iron,
tailings perhaps from a nearby mine.
He searched the tree line,
noted desiccated trees
fallen along the shore,
saw the beach eaten away,
a line of foam lapping at the sand.
He went out early,
fished until the fog
burned off, rested
in the morning stillness
until his bobber was lost
in the glint of early light.
He watched a loon
fish in the distance,
an eagle hunt above
the trees. His back, his shoulders
warmed to the sun like a box turtle
basking on a log. He removed
his vest, and sat there
watching the lake waken
like an old lover he'd completely
forgotten about.

On family vacations
in those early years growing up
that first glint of the lake
through the pines, the perfumed
breath of the northwoods

caused such excitement, built upon
a whole year's anticipation
for northern pike that fought
hard and long after countless hours
spent in an old wooden boat,
and once a muskie, not quite legal,
but still its eyes spun hate
and the treble hooks cut deep
into his hand as he unhooked
the long, angry muscle of fish—
a final lunge and it was gone,
and the years are gone, and the fish
smaller, the fishing more tedious,
more like a chore he put off doing
as a young boy until his mother
forced the issue on penalty of some restriction.

He no longer ties his own flies,
crafts his own lures; his reels,
once religiously cleaned and oiled,
now run gritty and dry.
And the hooks once sharpened
in that familiar ritual
repeated like a prayer season after season
now collect a dull corrosion.

One lone, unwanted crappie
brought the thought of cleaning,
gutting, washing knife and cutting board,
and even this reward for breakfast
consumed too much and so he let it go
and motored in to eggs, a soft chair,

a magazine slick with ads and articles
on how to make your money grow
and grow for years like this,
everything safe, and easy and comfortable,
money growing like duckweed
on his favorite, sheltered bay.

ICE BOWL

. . . the American people will no longer
tolerate the Vietnamese caring less about
winning than we do.
—U.S. Embassy official, reported 12/31/67

Frostbite is for losers.
—Vince Lombardi

After the officers course at Ft. Benning,
a stint as training officer
running various rifle ranges,
then a chemical warfare course
at McClellan, just outside
Anniston, Alabama, where
the orientation officer says
no one should be after dark—
Don't even stray off the main highway
he says, *It's not a good place to be,*
I get orders, a unit waiting
to be deployed to Viet Nam,
also not a good place to be,
December '67, and like they always said—
motto of the Army— *Hurry up and wait:*
we just sat there, more training,
and plenty of time to think about it,
so we got together and watched football,
lieutenants newly commissioned
including a grizzled former E-6 from Texas
with enough enlisted time for half a career,
part Indian, a Cowboys fan, and me
from Wisconsin— and the title game
was tight, thirteen below, wind chill

minus seventy, the field brittle as ice,
Dallas ahead by three
in the fourth, less than a minute
to go, ball on the one, and Donnie Anderson
can't move it a single inch against
the frozen Dallas line— two running plays
and nothing but time on the clock eaten up
until there's but sixteen seconds left
forcing Starr to call his final timeout:
he confers with Lombardi, says he can
sneak it past the goal though the coach
wants Mircein to punch it in:
Lombardi capitulates, says *Do it*
and let's get the hell out of here.
Starr, ever a master of deception,
calls Brown right, thirty-one wedge,
but the blocking assignments are the same
and Starr keeps the ball instead
of handing off to Mircein:
on the snap Kramer slams Jethro Pugh,
jams him outside just enough for Starr
to run through the gap, fall and
stretch across the goal: the Texan,
the Indian lieutenant, is crushed
like a beer can under a tank,
and I almost feel sorry for him:
as Tom Landry said after the game,
It was a dumb call
in a world filled with dumb calls
but elation knows little of mercy,
and next month there's Tet
a hard year for everyone,
not an inch of ground gained
in a losing season, no matter how

you look at it, and he didn't do well
when he came back, cold sweats
in a Texas heat wave, knees stiff from shrapnel,
bone shattered like ice, an unacceptable loss
where *Winning isn't everything*
he keeps telling himself
as the temperature falls,
as the wind—it must be the wind—
sends an icy chill down his back.

BOUNDARY WATERS

I can walk down a trail now—
an old portáge—
and not check out the branches
I push away from my face:
I still look down at the ground
and sometimes find myself stopping
to probe a well-placed pile of leaves,
an old log rotting and wet.
I notice the signs, shift
the weight of my pack.
Looking up to the sun
I bring myself back,
saying out loud to myself,
I doubt if the damned Potawatami
ever booby-trapped deer shit or bear,
and flick the stool over
with a stick, and laugh, and walk on.

Once, a year or two ago, through
kermi and rempi, I slipped, sunk
down in a natural hole, and I screamed
dreaming of punji stakes covered with feces
cutting into my ankle and calf.
I laughed, not even a sprain. But every
deer within miles lay down for the day.

It was like the week before deer season—
I'd see a dozen every morning and then nothing
on opening day.

But I'd be crazy to go out there then,
gunfire from every direction,
shooting at everything that moves,
better to wait—I have a crossbow—
accurate, camouflaged, and I can carry
a small deer for miles.

Before the shot
I ask for my breath to steady,
my eye to sight true,
my arrow to cut deep to the heart.
I thank the animal
for what he gives me,
for what I have learned.

There is so much wind today
the birds have not come out to feed.
I've watched blue jays, grackles, starlings
cut through snow—
the flakes heavy, shaken off their backs,
their wings, with a ruffle, almost a shiver
of cold—the way you'd feel in a Chinook
coming out of the heat to 3,000 feet,
or the sweat that chilled the back—
bracketed by mortars with so little cover,
no fall back defense.

Once, in elephant grass, rounds no more
than a foot overhead, we hit the ground hard
and fired, just inches above the hot, red earth—
and got a few, and they broke off:
an old E-6 who'd been through Korea
told us we'd have to *make like a snake*—
an old joke, but it worked.
Last spring I saw faces, camouflage,

the point of a recon team. The leaves
played tricks, the light, the time of year—
even the smell of earth and air brought it back.
I got down low, slid back, looked
for the logical ambush
along that avenue of approach. But it was
only the leaves, the thinking.

I don't see that now. I canoe
straight to the islands, set up camp,
lie awake listening to the stars,
the trees, the lake—sometimes a beaver
slaps his tail on the smooth water
when it's dark and I'm lying there
restless, unable to sleep—
the sound of a mortar round
hitting a half-drained paddy
on the other side of the world—
I turn over and it's almost easy to sleep.

FREE WILL, FIXED FATE, AND CHANCE

Lou Gehrig said he was the luckiest
man on the face of the earth when he retired:
and he probably was, as if luck
or chance had anything to do with it,
but the grace of that swing
did seem to have the imprint of heaven
on it, stamped into his bat like a trademark,
as if Gehrig had been ordained by the Almighty
to give mid-week sermons to the masses,
each containing parables we could understand,
lining them out one good hit after another,
every one an exemplar of virtue,
an article of faith.

But, what did Richie Ashburn ever do
to deserve his particular fate
when in August of '57
he fouled off a pitch low and outside,
and the ball sheared back and struck
Alice Roth in the face breaking her nose,
and what must Alice have done
to displease God, to incur such disfavor,
that just as she's being placed on a stretcher
to be taken out of the stands
to get her bloody nose bandaged,
Ashburn hits her again, another foul
off the end of his bat—another stinging rebuke:
all the symmetry, the geometry, the angles of baseball
brought into play, penance meted out,
heavenly justice for sins real and imagined.

SOMETHING LIKE A WAR

Ty Cobb said, *Baseball is something*
like a war, as if coming in with your spikes
sharpened and high were the equivalent
of flesh shredded by a fragmentation grenade
or a booby trapped 105 round. But the metaphor
doesn't hold. Even if Cobb raked his spikes
along the bone from ankle to knee
with a hard slide, or if Albert Belle
broke a shortstop's nose and dislocated
his shoulder running outside the base path
between second and third, it wouldn't be more
than a mild skirmish between two friends
drunk on a Saturday night and looking for trouble.
Any good player could always pick himself up,
dust his uniform off, and play the next day—
baseball is nothing like a war.

PLAYING CENTER IN MY FORTIES

With two balls, two strikes
I know he'll go after the next pitch
so I break to the third base side of second
as he pulls it, a sharp liner that tails away:
I dig in racing over the lumpy field,
legs pumping, glove outstretched
and then the snap, almost audible
as the ball just ticks the web of my glove.
I pull up lame as a horse with a broken leg—
as if I'd been shot or gotten a hot piece
of shrapnel burning into the back of my thigh.
I can't move, the pain so acute, so sharp
I feel the synapses arc like a short in a 220 line,
like a welding torch sparking through steel—
my breath breaks in short staccato gasps,
and I know this is it, this is some real
damage I can't just hobble away from
expecting to rest a couple of days
and then be back as good as new—not this time.
I know the muscle has ripped, torn jagged
like a piece of meat fought over
by a couple of hungry dogs;
the blood pumps, strains, filters through
meaty cells of muscle and flesh.
In a few days the back of my leg
turns a blackish-green, to blues and reds
spreading, changing color as the days pass.
Each halting step burns, and I walk
like an old man, but only for short distances
before my systems shut down
concentrating on the repair of this hamstring
and nothing else.

I lie back at night, wishing at least
that I'd made the catch, an easy play
just a few years before—
this is the warning shot across the bow,
the spotting round pinging the turret,
the caution lights flashing down the block:
warnings I pay no attention to
like a .220 hitter looking past the fence,
ignoring the coach's frantic signs
to lay down a bunt.

CANOEING QUETICO, 20 YEARS AFTER

After three days wind-locked
a break in the sky—
this long lake narrow as a pike
returns its placid face
once again to reflect
tall pines massively layered
against glacial rock formations—
there's a raven's mammoth beak,
a wildcat ready to spring,
a bear claw carved
above the shore.

It is easy to see
virtually anything;
memory, imagination, a fevered
chill in the morning breeze
conjure it all.

One wonders what the first explorers saw
across this bay so many ages past
where a lone campsite stirs,
and wood smoke rises like myth,
ancient stories that lift and break
into the pines. A hint of red
streaks like petroglyphs
across the sky.

I search for signs above the trees,
strain hard to see
if the wind will rise,
if this is just a moment's calm, a lull
before deep, explosive waves
build and threaten
my loaded canoe once again.

Clouds churn and spin
in this early morning light,
take shape, move quickly—
there's a flight of Hueys
skimming the trees,
noses angled down,
tails up like darting
dragonflies—

Dragonflies, here since before
the Paleocene, always here
outlasting everything, perhaps
even that flight of choppers
always there, passing overhead,
one combat assault after another
scudding across the years
holding on to the sky

and it won't let go.

A MEDITATION ON POLITICS AND BASEBALL

I used to think politics and baseball were separate
and apart like magnets we played with as kids—one
pole repulsing the other—no amount of pushing
could get the oppositional poles conjoined,
to touch—always a space between them.
With such naiveté we approach
the world, eternal optimism as opposed to a hard-
headed realism that works like a fastball
nicking a corner of the plate, that would serve us better,
no matter the issue, no matter the season,
no matter the game.

Ted Williams called President Truman
and Senator Taft *gutless politicians,* said
we hadn't half tried to win the Korean War.
Maybe Williams was right: maybe Truman.

A well hit ball makes everything else disappear:
a reason still to watch the game late
in a twilight double header.

But baseball seemed an anachronism in '72
when the Oakland A's played the Cincinnati Reds.
You would have thought the Reds would have changed
their name, given the politics of the time—
an embarrassment like supporting the Khmer Rouge
when Vietnam intervened in Cambodia, but, conversely,
the A's embodied the counter-culture,
long hair, handle bar moustaches,
an irreverence for duly constituted authority
whereas there were, as one sports writer wrote,
more crew cuts in Cincinnati than anyplace else

in America, all of them ready to take a baseball bat
to protesters in the street. Yet the scruffy A's won –
to the consternation of the right—Baseball,
America's pastime, taken over by the left,
a scruffy, bearded bunch of .250 hitters, and none
of them said we didn't try hard enough
to win in Vietnam.

FOXHEAD 400

. . . what did I know
of love's austere and lonely offices?
                    —Robert Hayden

I

In the cool of the cellar
a case—longneck bottles,
amber glass, and every night
just after my stepfather
took off jacket and tie
he'd open one—
a private ritual in a way
putting the work day behind—
another day, dollars already spent,
and the white shirt still starched,
French cuffs with maybe
just a gray touch
of pencil lead at the fold,
but he seldom talked
of the day at work, seldom
said anything of the hours,
the years, mounting up like bottles
you could maybe return
for a dollar or two
if only it were worth the time.

II

Time, when you're growing up
is so much different than when
you're older—days spread out

like summer trees shadowing the lawn,
and summer seems forever, time
for baseball, fishing, spinning tales,
and flying model airplanes.
Lost in books, one dreams of what the years
will hold in store, the days not scripted,
none the same as any other. So he seldom
talked about his day at work,
even when he brought work home.
Just once he mentioned something candidly
no boy could understand,
said he'd got his *ears burned,*
a small mistake, but costly,
even if it had been caught in time.

And youth is even less forgiving,
resistant to any authority,
so we argued, even in our play,
and he was still the faster of us both:
I couldn't escape; he was a star at track,
his record in the hurdles stood for years.

And yet, there was that time,
spring cleaning in the attic,
when we found his track shoes,
leather cracked and hardened in the attic heat,
and he said he'd often dreamed
of having a son someday
who would wear those shoes, an admission,
a revelation, I never felt or understood
until so many decades later,
long after his early death, long after his record
had been eclipsed.

III

When I was a little older and we went out
fishing after dark—the best time
for walleye, to put differences
aside—we'd suspend
shiners off some structure,
a drop-off where the big ones
came in late, and we'd wait
under the rising moon,
the lake still, the moon riding out
to the shore. Cottages—their yellow
lights—blinked like fireflies across the bay;
lanterns shivered at the end of a dock
where a few fishermen hauled in their catches,
cleaned them, gutted pumpkinseed
and bass while the fish stared up still alive,
gills respiring after death, a treat for the cats.

IV

And either we caught some or
we didn't, but one night I hooked
something so large it took the breath
of the moon away, fought its strong heart
until raised to the side of the boat—
a muskie or pike I couldn't tell—
it broke free, snapping the line
not strong enough to hold
its weight out of water—like so
much else I'd learn later—
and we just sat there
as the water quieted down, as the pock-marked
moon looked down with disinterest
having seen everything there is to see
a thousand times or more at least—

And we stopped fishing
for the night, motored in, went to a bar,
ordered a coke and a beer, and he started to say
what I should have done to get that fish in the boat,
but he stopped, knowing you never
recover what is lost, and what does it mean or matter
anyway, and some day we'd share this
over a couple of beers bottled in amber,
if it ever came time,
if ever the cold moon rose in our hearts—
all those years between us—
and burned like fire on the water.

BEHIND THE PLATE

Always the dumbest and fattest
kid played catcher—so slow
to first he was an easy out
even on a well hit grounder.
You had to be dumb, we thought,
to play that position—always the chance
of being hit with a foul tip
stinging face, hands, ankles
no matter how much protection,
and we didn't have much.
And too, it was best to be somewhat heavy
with thick arms and lumbering thighs
to take the bruise of an errant curve ball
sliced sharply off the plate
or a fast ball bounced wickedly into the groin.

So we were lucky to have someone
who wanted to catch,
and when the ball hit his knee with a hard crack,
he never complained. Always he would
walk it off, rubbing the sweat off his brow
with his sleeve. It was just part of the game,
like blocking the plate or taking one for the team.

Years later, if we ever thought about it,
we could still see him in his crouch
behind the plate, still see him going back
to the screen, ripping off his mask,
making certain catches of those high fouls
easily lost in the sun. And when he got his weight

into a pitch, he'd drive it deep,
broke a neighbor's window once
with a line drive so far back
no one even tried to make the catch.

And because he was dumb and slow
he worked for a year after high school,
got married, was drafted and sent to Asia
to play in the big leagues—a utility player,
one of the boonie rats sent to catch
the hardest game we'd ever played.
When he got the *Dear John* from his wife,
he called for a fast one high and tight,
and just like always he got hit,
the sting so sharp, so deep,
he wouldn't even try to walk it off.

TROPHIES

First warm night of spring
and junk week—
all those old stoves
and washing machines
that gave out during winter
are piled on the curb—
boxes of trash pulled down from
the attic, tires hauled up from the basement,
mildewed boxes of broken toys,
linoleum ripped up, soiled carpet,
a plastic garden hose hardened and cracked

One A.M. and I'm running, clearing
my head of a day thrown out
like the trash—a few junk pickers
are moving through the neighborhood
confident as thieves, finding another use
for objects other lives have discarded

Running down block after block
I notice a box
shining under a streetlamp—
a box filled with trophies
glittering into the night
like plastic and metal stars

I breathe harder
sucking spring air
into my lungs, aching, breaking
my stride—a box filled with trophies,
alone, next to the curb . . .

A green court under the lights,
the harsh sun, a man dressed in white
plays under that sun, those lights,
for years—winning and winning until
his life moves with the same
measure as the game,
until finally only the years win
and win again

A man known by his winning,
by hard won rules measuring out
the play of his life until now,
this hard long winter played out,
defeated finally by the rules it has made . . .

I run, pushing harder
into the dark,
sprint the last quarter
back home

Past box after box of trash
piled in front of house after house,
past that one house with that one box
filled with nothing but trophies—
so little left in this life to throw out.

ROWING BACK

Under a three-quarter moon
we rowed silently out
from the pier, the water motionless
as any prey or predator at night—
her parents, mine, unaware
of us out in the boat, on the lake
under that moon. I remember,
as you will too, how still
the water, how beautiful the light
on her face as I moved closer
for a watery kiss: Years later
my wife would caustically say,
You're a hopeless romantic—
strong emphasis on the word
hopeless and she's right. I still
dream of that kiss, that lake,
the moon streaming down
with all that parental worry
awaiting, as we knew,
as even you remember,
rowing back on that beam of light
to the punishing dock.

PLAYING BASEBALL IN THE ARMY: COMPANY PICNIC, 1967

We practiced for weeks
before playing the NCO's
at the company picnic,
and the colonel warned,
They've got a pitcher, Sergeant Simms,
who will put a spin on the ball
so tight all you'll do is pop up
to the infield—nine times out of ten.
And we did; we met Simms' arrogant proficiency
the way we met the ball,
one easy pop up after another—
until, in the middle innings,
I cut it hard, sent it bounding over third
and waltzed in for a double.
I looked at him and grinned.
You won't do that again, Lieutenant, he said,
but I did: Only I went the other way,
hit a sucker pitch
between first and second—had to slide
as the right fielder broke in on the ball
making it a close one, and the hard tag stung
leaving a welt for a week.
Simms didn't say anything, just stood on the mound
rubbing the ball into his glove,
but he handed me a beer after the game,
and we talked of the great games we'd seen,
the ones we'd played, of players who made
impossible plays. When he didn't come back
to his wife and son, the son he played catch with
after a long day on the ranges training recruits,
I remembered our company picnic, the game

we'd played that afternoon, and I still think
of those easy pop ups, his pitches fast,
burning across the plate, nicking the corners
except that one easy mistake, chest high,
seeming to hang like a grenade
daring me to hit it. And I still call out
to the mound, *Pitch it to me Sarge,*
make it a good one, come on, pitch to me.
The air, the fading sun, hangs heavy over the plate.

GOD WORKS IN MYSTERIOUS WAYS

If baseball were religion
solid contact with the ball
would be rapture, a sure ticket
to heaven, and running back
for a long fly, catching it
over the shoulder, would be such joy
that the Apostles would sing
and the wings of angels
would beat in your chest

So when a young woman I know
brings her small son to the desert
to watch baseball played
under a sky of endless blue—
spring training before the team
moves north for opening day—
she catches a future Hall-of-Famer
lazing to the field, asks him for an autograph,
a souvenir for the boy, and he says,
closing the gate behind him,
I can't, I have to get back to work

And the boy doesn't understand,
and the woman because the sky
is cathedral blue, and the outfield
shifts slowly, a few steps to the right
as the batter nonchalants the first pitch
and then weakly strokes a liner to short

And this is work
where the joy is gone
and the rapture doesn't play

and the sky burns a hole in your heart—
just another day at the office,
another day deep in the mines

She grabs her son by the hand,
walks back to her car, slides
across its hot vinyl seat.
On the road out of town
they drive past a small church
where men kneel at the altar,
make the sign of the cross,
and pray for work

ALL-STAR GAME 2008

Twelfth inning of the All-Star Game
and I'm nodding off,
missing pitches, an entire at bat.
By the bottom of the fifteenth
I've lost count, just want it to be over
though, philosophically, deep in my boyhood
psyche, I don't want it to end.
My body complains to my aging brain
We can't keep this up much longer.
Even my old friend baseball
can't keep me pinned to the screen.
Corey Hart goes back for a long fly,
makes a so-so throw to the plate
and the runner scores from third:
game over.

I flick off the digital receiver,
push the off button for the TV:
a flash of light from the TV screen
brightens the room.
It is like, I imagine, that last
flicker before I cease raging
against anything. But next morning
I wonder about that throw, two bounces
to the plate, think of high school wrestling,
the arm drag that drove my shoulder
into the mat, ripping muscle from bone,
making it hard to throw even a hundred feet
thereafter: always a wince, a sharp sting
coursing down the arm. I regret the usual
misunderstanding, how so many fans
focus on hitting or those extraordinary catches

of well hit balls: over the shoulder catches,
balls caught leaping, reaching over
the fence, the diving catch of a line drive
spiraling away from the fielder, arcing
to the ground only to be snared in the webbing,
an ice cream cone as they say, the fielder
raising it above his head, proof for the umpire
who signals an out. That's all well and good,
but it's what comes after, like an afterthought,
with a runner on base: the throw to prevent
the runner's advance.

It is the throw
I believe in, its perfect trajectory,
its beauty as it nails the runner stretching
for second, running for home.
It is the perfection of what is taken
for granted, most often ignored or discounted,
the way we dismiss those bare elements
of our lives, ungraciously accepting the beauty
of a simple and elegant transference:
energy, love, power, justice, accuracy—
a certain death for defiance
of what's thought ordinary and commonplace.

TRIPTYCH

FITNESS

At the gym— I'm sorry—the Fitness Center, the music is ubiquitous, mindless as muzak, designedly less than misogynistic for the female clientele. Men look at women (their bare legs spread wide on the hip adduction machine) surreptitiously out of the corners of their eyes. A woman's bare shoulder reveals a tattoo: *The sun is always rising in the sky somewhere.* I want to tell her she's wrong; her model of the solar system is in error; the sun does not rise anywhere, on this or any other planet, regardless of tidal locking. I wonder, working a machine mindlessly, what else she believes that's wrong. Surely this is not her only error, error defining the paradigm of our lives. And my error? Whatever I believe is true today is true today only. I pose a philosopher's lament, not knowing the certainty of my way. I watch a line of men and women walking fast and hard on a regimented line of treadmills. We are slaves to our machines said Thoreau slavishly tending a row of beans. I think of my own thirty years working, a silly drumbeat in my ear. Just twenty reps, twenty, on this machine and I am done.

THE LOTUS TATTOO

She has the tattoo of a lotus on her shoulder, an inscription in Chinese on her right side running along her ribs, visible only when she raises her arms on the iso-lateral shoulder press machine; she must have shaved this morning. I know I shouldn't stare and thusly adhere to the two Mississippi rule, looking away after the second Mississippi and then looking back again, my appreciation as long, as deep, as the river. Her shoulders are broad, like those of a swimmer, her waist narrow, and though all women my age have seen their waists change with childbirth, with the long passing of years, this woman works out believing there will never be a change, impervious to the evidence as we all thought, as we all must. She knows surely that an old man's lust or even a benign desire is despicable, and yet she must discern, as well, that the despised male gaze is that of a man admiring a painting in the Louvre, perhaps a woman in her bath, shoulders blossoming with the warmth—and so much easier to be a painter than a poet, no explanation necessary, and easier still to be a geographer mapping the contours of a new found land. The ancient cartographers, the Old Masters, knew— as she must know— with each lift, her shoulders burn for the ages.

BALTIMORE ORIOLES AND AMERICAN CIVILIZATION

There are stories of Earl Weaver standing buck naked in the clubhouse after a close game, discussing the finer points, the finesse so much a part of baseball, talking to reporters who subsequently wrote everything wrong. I remember an afternoon of squash and afterwards standing in the locker room naked and still wet from a shower talking to a professor, similarly naked, about the paper I was writing and my work as TA for his course in American Civilization, all manner of thought and inquiry on the most wondrously fascinating academic concerns. He died a short time ago, passed on as did Weaver, and I think of them both naked in the locker room, how all great things are thought and spoken in the nude—decisions to marry, to have children, entire courses of our lives determined, a celebration of the pure physical joy of being, and, often, explanations of why we make the substitutions we do, the changes, those wild decisions going against the percentages that never make sense to anyone else. The lesson, I believe, is to be naked for everyone to hear.

ALUMINUM II

At a run-down resort
built just before the war—
an old fishing camp turned into cabins
with a beach cleared for the children—
not much upgrading in forty years,
but now, taken over by a young couple
bringing it back, new log cabins
replace the old, their roofs swaybacked
and overgrown with lichen and moss.
Along the beach sleek aluminum craft
replace rotting, wooden row boats
no one has launched in years:
waterlogged, a few are overturned
in the tree line back from the beach, moss-covered,
gray wood exposed under the paint—
several so far gone only the ribs remain.
In the fish-cleaning shack a few wooden lures
hang in a snaking line down the wall,
linked each to each by treble hooks rusted and blunt.

Now, nothing rots or rusts—monofilament tangles
in the feet, strangles ducks and raccoon:
once, old beer cans glinted in the shallows for a short time
then wasted to nothing; now, aluminum cans
stay flashing the light summer after summer,
their pop-tops glittering along the bottom
like lost spoons or spinner baits.

I take a new silver boat hot from the sun
out on the lake to either dream or fish,
and in the quiet of late afternoon
I listen to harsh sounds of waves

clunking against the boat
scattering whatever fish are lurking nearby,
and the sound is different, the pleasant
music of water lapping against those old green
wooden boats has changed, in pitch and timbre;
and other sounds have changed as well—
no more puttering one-and-a-half horse
fishing motors that took an hour to cross the lake.

I hike to one of the old cabins moved out back
away from the new log home built in its place,
walk past the lopsided timbers sagging from years
of neglect and long winters, look in a window
and see a fisherman sitting at a log table
taking apart his bait casting reel,
oiling the parts, rigging braided cotton line
of at least 30 lb. test and a steel leader.

Might as well mourn the loss of ritual
in the church I say to myself and
the chastising squirrel overhead.
I pick up my musty Duluth pack,
shift its weight on my shoulders,
place the thwart of an old wooden canoe
back of my neck and portáge to a lake
that freezes over completely by late fall.

I take a few strokes with my paddle
then drift slowly in the slight breeze
from one end of the lake to the other;
I move in and out of the bays,
circle a small island that's nothing but bog.

I fish a dummy lure all day,
an old Basserino, its red and white paint
chipped off and nearly gone, casting it perfectly
along weed beds and fallen trees, varying
its retrieve, sharing the laugh with a surfacing loon
trilling hysterically just off my bow.

THE AIR FORCE PLAYS BASEBALL
NEAR THE SOUTH CHINA SEA

—for Fred Kiley, Col., USAF, ret.

He tells me a barrage of 8-inch guns
moves a battleship sideways, leaving
a vast plain of smooth water behind,
glassy smooth, a pane of blue
reflecting clouds, the cordillera where
white puffs burst like flowers
after a warm spring rain. And once,
playing baseball, the count 3 and 2
a mortar round bursts in the outfield
far out in left, no immediate danger
as they walk in the rounds, and the batter
wants the next pitch, and no player
wants the game called
on account of enemy fire;
the right fielder doesn't even look
nervously over his shoulder
as the next round explodes
in reaches of elephant grass
while the next takes out a stand
of bamboo. The catcher sets up, gives
the sign and location, outside
because the batter is stocky and short,
with powerful arms that will drive in
the runners on second and third. Another round
sings through the trees as the batter
digs in at the plate, red dirt
clumping on his boots,
and the pitcher warns the runners back
with a glance, almost a balk as the mortar

opens up, and an 8-inch round blossoms
just yards from that mortar crew set up
in a high cave overlooking the field,
and the next round hits the entrance
to this cave as the hillside collapses
into itself, a perfect strike, like the pitch
the batter whiffs swinging for his life,
and the side is out, smoke moving
in the wind down the mountains
like early morning mist.
The outfield saunters in
holding on to their lead;
the stranded runners pick up their gloves,
become lost in circles of smoke
dissipating, disappearing,
like VC vanishing into the brush;
they set up in the outfield, wait
as the pitcher warms up tossing a few,
as the hitter steps into the box.
He looks to the green pleasure beyond them,
as if the fielders, as if the enemy,
weren't even there.

AN ESSAY ON ZERO TOLERANCE

My daughter, barely three, is at the age of play,
and I'm at work teaching a night course,
trying to be human when the humanities
prove the least humane of all our academic disciplines.
I document our silly prevarications,
our penchant for error: as Yogi Berra said
We made too many wrong mistakes—no matter
how many lessons we've been taught.
So when I return home from the university
I find she has a cast on her leg, a deep
fluorescent pink, as if color mitigates
the break. Even today she still loves
fluorescent colors: backpack, running shoes
glowing in the dark. Tibia fractured,
the doctor looks askance; it's the second
bone she's broken. Examining X-rays he asks her
how it happened: I've been told the story,
how her mother told her not to jump
from the play set in the park onto the hard
playground surface, this in the days
before swing sets were removed by cautious
legislators, and recycled tires were ground into
a softer surface. But she jumped anyway,
clowning, laughing, her knees locked, jumped despite
her mother's admonition, as we all do, as we did
to become who we are, separate, playing
apart from parents, from anyone
insisting otherwise, even our gods
created as reflections of ourselves:
Manjushri, god of wisdom, always warring
with the god of doing something dumb.
I jumped stupid, my daughter said,

admitting a fault, admitting the right
to do the wrong thing because so many rules
are foolish, and we have before us
so many fabled adults who misbehave, history
the record of that misbehavior.
So if there's a lesson here, it lies inside
that fluorescent cast, a break that teaches
we do wrong regardless, and who's to tell us
there's any other way to live, to learn,
to jump for joy, even if it is stupid.

AUKER'S LAMENT

Everybody asks me about baseball, and I was
only in that about 10 years, but I was in the
abrasive business about 30 some years, and
no one ever asks me anything about abrasives.
—Elden Auker

That's just the way it is:
I've been in the abrasive
business myself for more than 30 years.
Every time I walk into the classroom
I rub someone raw. If students come in
unmarked and leave without an abrasive
burn or two, like sliding naked
into second base on a diamond mined
with gravel and broken glass,
I haven't done my job.

But I'd much prefer to talk about
baseball, the way the ball curves
across the plate just begging to be hit,
that feel in the hands as the ball drives deep,
Magnus forces affecting its flight.
There's nothing in the classroom—
no philosophy, no politics,
no art, not even metaphysics
of the ball being hit
that can sing like that.
Ideas are sandpaper,
and no matter the grit,
no matter the application,
they wear down faster
than any game we've ever played.

MOTHER TERESA PLAYS TENNIS

It's hard to play tennis and be
Mother Teresa at the same time.
—Maria Sharapova

It is a philosophy of sport,
the killer instinct
take no prisoners approach;
as my wrestling coach would say,
Punish your opponent, make him hurt,
push his face into the mat.
Once in tennis class
I hit the corners so beautifully
with every shot, my opponent, angry
as if I'd stolen his girlfriend
or keyed his new car,
frustrated at being yanked from one side
of the court to the other, yelled,
It's only practice, you can't learn
anything if you do that—he meant
succeed at playing the game of course.
So I let up and we didn't learn anything.

Another time, playing squash, I had
an opponent who said, being English,
he was at a disadvantage with the American ball,
could we play with the softer English ball, slower
than ice melt on Pluto and, of course, my timing was off—
might as well have played with a nerf ball—
and when he won he regarded me
with such venal disdain, because the game wasn't that close,
or, more likely, because I'd fallen for his ruse.

I imagine Mother Teresa having a wicked
backhand, topspin keeping the ball
low, as if the net weren't even there—
seldom an unforced error,
her white habit flowing across the court,
opponents kept back of the baseline,
her game played like a prayer.

Christy Mathewson would not
grant interviews to sports writers
who cheated on their wives.
Today he'd have to take a vow of silence,
novitiate nuns in a convent permitted to talk more.

And Walter Johnson never threw
the brush back, chin music not the way
to play his game, so when a batter,
say Ty Cobb, crowded the plate
Johnson threw outside; Cobb took
advantage and whaled on Johnson's kindly nature.

Carl Mays, Ty Cobb, Albert Belle, all mean
and disagreeable, hot tempered,
spikes high, bean ball, forearm to the throat,
a Machiavellian philosophy of sport.
Might as well watch wrestling on TV, though
there the meanness at least is fake.

Mother Teresa admitted she had doubts;
those who don't are the ones
to worry about. My daughter tested faith
playing soccer, outfoxing her opponents
she was tripped when about to score:
then a girl— schooled in meanness— deliberately

stepped on her outstretched hand, twisting
her foot as it came down hard. The coach
said her finger wasn't broken
despite the bone angling crazy in all directions:
of course it wasn't broken; if it were
there would be paper work, or maybe the coach
was consumed by faith, good works
merely a niggling concern.

It's all right I used to say—scraped
knee, bruised feelings, tibia fractured
on the playground, gym teacher never throwing her the ball
despite the fact the boys couldn't catch it.
It's all right, I'd say, *It's gonna be all right.*
I'd sing these lines over the years adding a bluesy note
to growing up. After the bones were set,
after months of physical therapy,
her finger still juts at crazy angles
and she did lose faith, at least she didn't play
competitively again.
Maybe that's the wrong lesson,
maybe that's what you have to learn.
Nixon voiced it best: . . . *that is the time*
to get tough, to kick the guys in the balls!
That's what they won't do. That's
what I always do. Lefty Grove
wrote that book before Nixon; during
batting practice he threw at his own teammates.

Reading the morning paper as a young boy,
I'd turn to the sports page looking for
the box score that told me
what Joe Adcock, first baseman for the Braves,
had done the night before, and I was stunned,

let down because he charged the mound,
chased Ruben Gomez into the stands. But
this wasn't Cobb on a racial rant,
this was Adcock, thrown at constantly
to diminish his threat, his power,
his standing in the record books.
It's a good thing I didn't catch him, Adcock said,
though at times, over the years, I've wished he had.
When Gomez died I felt no remorse.

But that is the wrong lesson, the wrong
reasoning, a wicked parable of loss.
Running back on a long fly,
that instant the ball is captured in the glove
like some Zen satori awakening,
and the fade away jump shot, moving
back from one's opponent, a moment of
nonresistance, something St. Francis would espouse.

My wife was an all-city guard
back when girls were seldom allowed
on the court. (Still there are men who say
court time is wasted on women.)
We used to go to the playground
and shoot buckets, an easy game
of H-O-R-S-E. Maybe that's all it's worth,
play for the sake of play, like Mother Teresa
caring for the poor, nothing comes of it,
all those needs can never be met, there will
always be poor, though we keep trying,
the ball, after a long volley,
driven hard into the net.

THE OUTFIELD COMING HOME

No place, no position
ever suited a man more
than the outfield suited him—
always he had played deep,
often in center, sometimes in right
where he could watch the game
and move with the game's movement
until years of study had him
moving even before the pitch was hit
to the place the ball would be,
and his long strides took him
to that point of intersection
where the ball sunk deep into the pocket
with the sound and feel that everything was right
no matter what else there was in the world,
a knowledge that this was the one right thing
this man could do.

In less than two years an early out
brought him back to the game
where he noted the uneven field
for the first time, the ground giving way
as he ran back, his knee giving out
in a slight depression, breaking his stride,
and when the ball nicked the web of his glove
and bounced off for extra bases,
he felt the awkwardness of running it down,
throwing off line with a hurried throw
back to the infield, the cutoff man
having to chase his errant throw.
And when he twisted his ankle
late in a game in mid-summer

going back for a routine fly
that caught him just as he caught
the edge of a freshly dug gopher hole,
he felt the sharp edge of the world give way,
dissolving like the certainty of a catch.

Whatever else he did caromed at crazy angles
or skittered beyond reach of his glove.
It don't mean nothin' he tried
to tell himself as he ran in
on a line drive that kept rising
until it sailed over his head
and rolled all the way to the fence.

And just so, whatever he had learned
over all those years, so sure and straight,
was uneven like the ground he played on,
the air shimmering above the diamond,
the light playing tricks,
and that one sure thing lost in the sun.

COYOTE SANGHA

From the north, northwest
a play of light and shade:
thermals awaken;
cloud shadows snake
down and along
these canyon walls,
bare faces of rock, pine
struck at oblique angles
to the crumbling stone—
freeze and thaw a process
that cuts and rives, carves
switchbacks that change
perspective with each step.

When I break from the trail
a desert toad hops under
some brush; carpets of brown
needles cushion each step.
A mule deer just stares at my approach
then bolts into the blessing of pine,
the piety of refuge.
Everywhere else it is still:
I want a temple to magically appear
near the top of this perilous slope
almost floating in the low hanging
clouds. I want this a sangha
or sanctuary from reason,
from a phalanx of unyielding knowledge.

Circling back, I follow a light-dance
in the descent, the fluid dance of a shaman
working a cure. I stop on an outcrop, piles

of expended .45 ACP, hundreds of shells,
evidence of an afternoon shoot. I wonder
why the shooter didn't bother, didn't care,
to police his brass.

Later that night, unable to calm
I push hard on a tiring run.
A coyote's black shadow
disappears into heavy brush, cuts through
as I spin to catch him crossing the street,
the streetlamp following his jaunt
up into the hills, the Front Range:
this is the process of withdraw and return,
the eternal grace of resurrection.
Follow me, he says; *the temple lies ahead*
just below that blossoming moon.

CECROPIA

Maybe six, maybe seven—
I had just that many years—
I discovered a wildly magnificent Cecropia moth,
wings open, bigger than my hands, attached
to the porcelain tiles decorating the façade
of the building that housed my father's business.
Years later, many years after my father died,
I met several businessmen, his competitors,
and they told me how good a businessman he was,
astute and clever, exceptional in what he did.
It seemed they were envious of his commercial talent;
possessed of such they might have made a fortune.

I have the business sense of a brick.

But I knew the beauty of that moth, the huge
eyes marking its wings, a mask frightening
in the aspect of those eyes redolent with menace, just daring
any predator to chance its fate.

In college, evolutionary biology, I learned
the virtue of such adaptations,
such power to control.

My mother took the moth I'd carefully removed—
so very little wing dust on my hands—
and spread its wings upon the office wall,
then pinned it, wax paper covering its pulsing wings
so it could not breathe. I watched it,
its beauty, felt remorse and dread,
its wings attempting to respire.

Framed on a bed of cotton, it hung
on my bedroom wall for years, colors captured,
its antennae like fronds of eyelash,
a daily reminder of the sacred wonders
in our world.

Years later, rough-housing, wrestling,
a tag team match in my bedroom,
I was nearly pinned and kicking to be free:
the Cecropia crashed to the floor,
frame and glass breaking, and the brittle wings
broke like stained glass windows
of a church, a basilica, blown out by war,
like the Cathédrale de Notre Dame de Rouen, all
those brilliant blues and reds scintillant
in the sun, destroyed by allied bombing,
the detonating velocity of those bombs greater
than 1600 meters per second, a firestorm
that seemed the wrath of God.

Later, wrestling in high school, struggling
to make weight, I moved quickly, surely
on the mats and lost: eleven pounds
too much to lose on my skinny 120 pound frame.
But I loved the sport, the economy of a switch,
the viper-like strike of a single-leg take down,
the cross-face and quick spin around the body
to gain control. But I shiver at remembrance
of that struggle to lose and then maintain
that weight for an entire season,
weight a fierce competitor, more so
than any wrestler on the mats.

One morning, no real food for days,
I woke and stumbled to the floor,
my chest tight, breath labored,
my respiration slowed—like that moth
upon the wall. Too weak to wrestle,
I fell asleep that afternoon and missed the chartered bus,
that evening's match. Next day, Coach, example at hand,
kicked me off the team. Explanations of no avail,
just another lesson, like another move, I had to learn.

But explanations seldom work:
reason its own impasse, logic an impediment,
experience the same. I've thought through this for us both,
the many takedowns and reversals since,
our fortunes and misfortunes linked,
both of us pinned against
the unearthly beauty of this world.

SELFIE

A friend says, "Baseball is boring,"
reflecting a common cultural prejudice,
"a thing between pitcher and hitter
while everyone else stands around.
There's no movement, as if stone statuary
or carved chess pieces
are cemented in the outfield." The night before
he watched an entire game where nothing
was ever hit to right field.
He wonders what that fielder thinks about
during the game. I tell him,
"Ted Williams used to think
about hitting, the nuances of every
pitch, every pitcher given to
idiosyncratic tells, a forecast
of what's coming." My football-addicted
friend says he doesn't like basketball either,
though fast paced, high scoring:
all the games are alike.
I recall another friend, Army Captain,
Vietnam veteran, a Texas man who loved football
more than God or country or life itself.
Season over, descending into that lame time—
limbo of uncertainty and discontent—
we went to a Baltimore Bullets game
with nothing else to do while awaiting
reassignment. After a hard-won fade away
hitting nothing but net, he says, "I just don't like
watching all those big black men
racing down the court." I was a newly
minted second lieutenant and said
nothing in reply. The war changed us.

Football is all there is—all that hitting,
the taking of enemy ground,
the punishment of one's adversary. I know
that level of intimidation; as a teenager
playing football in the backyard, I came off
the line and hit a neighbor's father
hard. He backed off on every play
thereafter. Still, baseball holds its ground,
the thrill of a base hit, a great catch
running down a well hit ball, and yet,
summer game over, the eternal abiding cold
dug into my joints, I'm almost ashamed
at the revel I feel when an opponent is knocked
senseless on a winning drive, brain swollen
against the bone, a concussion
that will leave him thinking, wondering,
It was worth it, it was worth it
years later when he stumbles across the living
room to watch a game on TV.

FISHING NEAR WINTER

This is my last adventure of the year,
my last voyage before the lake freezes
and the roads are closed. Cold settles,
layers in, over this northern Minnesota lake
mimicking my bulky, cumbersome coat
worn over a thick sweater and a heavy woolen shirt.
My boots, also thick and heavy, clunk against
the bottom of the boat. Every cast,
every retrieve, causes my fingers
to numb, lake water soaking
my fingerless gloves, and the fish
wet my clothes increasingly with each catch.
A squall descends on the lake, feathery snow
that looks deceptively like down. Lake and sky
are monochromatic, an Impressionist's
nightmare. It is hard to speak in the cold,
and yet the cold pales with what's to come.
I think of Shackleton trapped in the ice,
of climbers who froze only a matter
of meters from the summit. Their desiccated bodies
lie there still. One must have the mind
of winter to know the joy of dragonflies
at the end of the rod, dancing in the sun,
living the life that comes, is sure to come.
Wait for it, as it lies waiting
bedded down for the night.

SPRING RIDE

Along the bike trail
Fresh mounds of dog shit: 110
PSI—squish, squish.

Many thanks to Professor Eric Gadzinski for his article
on the baseball and Vietnam poems entitled
*"The Hardest Game We'd Ever Played: Baseball as Metaphor in Four Vietnam
War Poems By Dale Ritterbusch"*
Published in *Aethlon: The Journal of Sport Literature*
Volume XXV: 1, Fall 2007/Winter 2008

The author of this manuscript is well aware that various records referred to in these poems have since been broken and that historical information has been eclipsed by the passage of time.

The author may be reached at the following address:
206 Spring Street
Waukesha, WI 53188
ritterbd@uww.edu

D. E. Ritterbusch is the author of several previous collections of poetry including *Far From the Temple of Heaven* and *Lessons Learned: Poetry of the Vietnam War and its Aftermath* based on his military experience as an officer in the U. S. Army. He was twice selected to be the Distinguished Visiting Professor in the Department of English and Fine Arts at the United States Air Force Academy and recently retired after a long career as a Professor of English at the University of Wisconsin-Whitewater. His creative and scholarly work has been archived in the Department of Special Collections on the imaginative representations of the Vietnam War at La Salle University in Philadelphia. He has published hundreds of poems and prose pieces in various periodicals, and his work has been dealt with in various books, articles, conference presentations, and dissertations. He was awarded an $8,000 Wisconsin Arts Board grant for his book *Lessons Learned*. He has a profound hearing loss which the Veterans Administration admitted is the result of military service. He lives in his hometown, Waukesha, Wisconsin, and winters in Surprise, Arizona.

Into the Cross-Walk